"This is a story every student and worker should read. Although the events Robichaud recounts happened long ago, women and other feminized people encounter similarly dismissive attitudes and ongoing intransigence about workplace sexual harassment today. This riveting account gives us hope and ammunition to not just protect the gains of the past, but to also expand the fight for justice in the present."

—SUSAN FERGUSON, author of *Women and Work: Feminism, Labour, and Social Reproduction*

"*It Should Be Easy to Fix* is an important look beyond the headlines of Bonnie Robichaud's groundbreaking court victory. A working-class mother from Northern Ontario, she is the unlikely hero of this story. Yet in these pages, she powerfully details how she remained steadfast in her belief that a safe workplace was her right. Canadian women are safer as a result of her sacrifice."

—JULIE S. LALONDE, author of *Resilience Is Futile: The Life and Death and Life of Julie S. Lalonde*

"This landmark Supreme Court decision remains extremely important in the context of the #MeToo movement and harassment suits against the RCMP and within the military. In *It Should Be Easy to Fix*, Bonnie Robichaud tells her story in intimate detail. The book should be required reading for all interested in ending gender-based harassment. Thank you, yet again, Ms. Robichaud, for your courage."

—NADIA VERRELLI and LORI CHAMBERS, authors of *No Legal Way Out: R v Ryan, Domestic Abuse, and the Defence of Duress*

"*It Should Be Easy to Fix* documents Bonnie Robichaud's courageous and dedicated advocacy to have the Supreme Court recognize workplace sexual harassment in Canadian law. She shows us how much advocates risk to change oppressive systems. We are all indebted to Bonnie Robichaud."

—MANDI GRAY, post-doctoral associate, University of Calgary

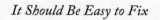

It Should Be Easy to Fix

It Should Be Easy to Fix
Bonnie Robichaud

Between the Lines
Toronto

It Should Be Easy to Fix
© 2022 Bonnie Robichaud

First published in 2022 by
Between the Lines
401 Richmond Street West, Studio 281
Toronto, Ontario · M5V 3A8 · Canada
1-800-718-7201 · www.btlbooks.com

Library and Archives Canada Cataloguing in Publication

Title: It should be easy to fix / Bonnie Robichaud.
Names: Robichaud, Bonnie, author.
Description: Includes index.
Identifiers: Canadiana (print) 2021038459X | Canadiana (ebook) 20210384611 |
    ISBN 9781771135887 (softcover) | ISBN 9781771135894 (EPUB) |
    ISBN 9781771135900 (PDF)
Subjects: LCSH: Robichaud, Bonnie. | LCSH: Sexual harassment—Law and
    legislation—Canada. | LCSH: Sexual harassment of women—Law and
    legislation—Canada.
Classification: LCC KE3256.W6 R63 2022 | LCC KF3467 .R63 2022 kfmod |
    DDC 344.7101/4133—dc23

Cover photograph by Jessica Deeks
Cover and text design by DEEVE

Printed in Canada

We acknowledge for their financial support of our publishing activities: the Government of Canada; the Canada Council for the Arts; and the Government of Ontario through the Ontario Arts Council, the Ontario Book Publishers Tax Credit program, and Ontario Creates.

To my sweet husband, Larry.
To my children, Darren, Kathleen, Jeff, Adrian, and Paul.
To my supportive friend Yvonne.

CONTENTS

The Honorable Claire L'Heureux-Dubé

B ONNIE ROBICHAUD IS AN EXTRAORDINARY WOMAN WHO against all odds at the time did what she thought was the right thing to do and, also against all odds, did win one of the most important legal rights not only for herself but for all other persons (mostly women) whose right to be treated with dignity by their employer was at stake.

I was sworn in as a Justice of the Supreme Court of Canada on May 4, 1987. Two days later, on May 6, I was sitting on the bench with six other members of the court, hearing the case of Bonnie Robichaud and the Canadian Human Rights Commission v. Her Majesty the Queen as represented by the Treasury Board ((1987) 2 s.c.r. 84).

The case, as stated in the Supreme Court's report, reads as follows: "Mrs. Bonnie Robichaud filed a complaint with the Canadian Human Rights Commission dated January 26, 1980, that she had been sexually attacked, discriminated against and intimidated by her employer, the Department of National Defence, and that Dennis Brennan, her supervisor, was the person who had sexually harassed her."

In a unanimous decision of the court, rendered on July 29, 1987, Justice La Forest, writing for the court, explained what was the issue the court had to deal with as follows:

"The issue in this case is whether an employer is responsible for the unauthorized discriminatory acts of its employees in the course of their employment under the Canadian Human Rights Act s,c 1976-77, c.33 as amended."

The court reached the following conclusion:

> A supervisor's responsibilities do not begin with the power to hire, fire, and discipline employees, or the power to recommend such actions. Rather, a supervisor is charged with the day-to-day supervision of the work environment and with ensuring a safe, productive workplace. . . . it is precisely because the supervisor is understood to be clothed with the employer's authority that he is able to impose unwelcome sexual conduct on subordinates.

Bonnie Robichaud had won a long and difficult battle.

It was all about discrimination by employers against employees that, on account of employers' denial of their responsibilities and liability, forced employees with little resources generally, to devote time and efforts, with at times discouraging obstacles, to resort to the courts to obtain justice which they were entitled to.

So important was this case, so difficult had it been to get there, and so improbable was the result at that time that the whole story of this search for justice had to be told: Bonnie Robichaud is now telling it in her own words. Her resilience, her faith in justice, and her own sense that she could not let this attack on her dignity be without sanction had triumphed: Bonnie Robichaud had made law. You will find her long road to justice, the numerous obstacles she encountered on the way, the help she got to get there, and the spirit that animated her all along both inspiring and fascinating.

Bonnie Robichaud is my hero.

INTRODUCTION

"It Should Be Easy to Fix"

M Y STORY AT ITS BEGINNING IS SIMILAR TO THAT OF SO MANY women in the workforce of the 1970s faced with being fired or having to quit because of sexual harassment.

I was married with five children, born only about a year or so apart, and was working at part-time, minimum-wage jobs, with hours that suited the employer and without protection. As a family, it was hard to make ends meet. With my income we were just about able to stay ahead of the bills.

When I finally found work as a unionized cleaner for the federal government at a Department of Defence military base, it felt really good. October 3, 1977, was the day I started working there. The position was complete with regular hours, benefits, sick days, and vacation pay. I knew it was a job I could do well. What I had not envisioned as part of the job was my boss's constant mental and physical pressure to have a sexual relationship, not to mention the discrimination, simply for being a woman.

In 1979, faced with failing my six-month probation, being fired if I complained, or quitting, I decided it did not have to end that way. I was going to fight.

This book is written mostly about events in the 1980s, based on notes I took at the time and on my memory, often confirmed with the public record. Inevitably, though, at this distance in time, there will be inconsistencies, and any errors are my responsibility. It is a story of my eleven-year struggle, the exhilarating occasional ups and the long, desperate downs of fighting for my job and for my sexual harassment complaint to be heard. In 1979, I filed a formal complaint and, in 1987, took it all the way to the Supreme Court of Canada. I won the fight and changed the law.

When I started, I had no idea how widespread sexual harassment was in the workplace. When a high-ranking officer said I was the only one who had ever complained, I said, "Good, then it should be easy to fix."

I

My Life Before

I WAS BORN APRIL 14, 1945, IN THE NETHERLANDS, AND WHEN I was seven years old, my family sailed by ship to immigrate to Canada. My mother, who was thirty before she had her first child, brought me and my then six siblings, one still in diapers, to Halifax, and then on to Toronto by train, no small feat. My father had arrived six months ahead of the rest of the family to prepare for our arrival.

Like so many others, my parents had decided to move to Canada to give us a better life with more opportunities. They worked hard as new Canadians, and life at home was not easy. My father started his own business selling mostly Dutch food imports, which meant he was away from home two weeks out of four, taking orders all around southeastern Ontario. My mother had two more children after we immigrated, making me the fourth child of nine, with six sisters and two brothers.

I took what felt like a long time to learn English, about three years before I could speak comfortably to anyone. This made a big difference in my early years, both socially and with my education. English gave me a lot of trouble with grammar and spelling.

My mother was very strict and had tight reins on us. As a teenager, by the time I got through telling her where I was going and when I would be back, it wasn't worth going out at all. Finally, I just stopped going places. I saw what happened when my sister didn't get home on time. It took years, even after I moved out and was married, before I realized I could just go out when I wanted.

I first began to work outside the house when I was about eleven or twelve, delivering the *Globe and Mail* newspaper. I did well with it and once I was even chosen carrier of the month and won a three-day trip to New York City.

The paper route began at 5 a.m., and one morning I had a man show up and expose himself when I was picking up my bundle of papers. I told my mom about it, and she called the police who followed me and found him. It didn't affect my delivering papers, and I just continued to deliver them. At home we didn't talk about what happened after that, and there was nothing at home or school to prepare me for inappropriate sexual behaviour. Sex was just not talked about at home. I'd say, my sex education amounted to my mom giving me a book about periods shortly after mine began, and in school we were told not to have sex because of venereal diseases.

In high school, I did well enough at my studies, but was too shy to make friends. School was two miles away and, for the first two years, I would ride my bike. I felt good about this. It saved me a lot of time and effort—the books were heavy! During those two years, the common dinner-table discussion was of me as one of only three girls at a high school of fifteen hundred students who rode a bike to school.

At some point I worked in a grocery store, and then, after graduating from high school, I worked in a bakery. It was heavy work and long hours, with no paid overtime. I earned one dollar an hour, the male university student, two dollars per hour, and the older man was paid four dollars per hour. I noticed that I had a wider range of duties than all of the others. I did more and was paid less.

I could have stayed there full time, but having graduated high school I felt sure I could do better. After a three-month stay in a job where, I heard later, they would lay off a lot of staff just before their three-month probation ended to get out of paying benefits, I found a job with the Ontario Department of Highways (now the Ontario Ministry of Transportation and Communications). This job had steady hours and pay, and I was making more than at the bakery or the three-month job. I worked in the typing pool and then, with a promotion, I moved over to personnel records. It was a good time and a good job.

ROMANCE

While I was working at the ministry, I met my future husband. Larry had been working in Sudbury at the same ministry and was transferred to the office in Toronto in October 1965. Larry's first wife had passed away the January before he was transferred. He worked as an office clerk on contracts, grants, and subsidies to the municipalities. Maybe I noticed him, but I pretty well ignored him when he first arrived. Mildred Swartz, who worked near Larry, kept telling him he should ask me out, and after several days of that he did. Larry had said I was too young, twenty to his thirty-three years.

Near the end of January, I was surprised by a phone call from him in the evening. He told me to put my hand in my pocket. For once, I hadn't put my hand in my pocket that whole day. When I looked, I found that he had written a poem on an adding machine tape, and he asked me out.

On our first date Larry took me to the O'Keefe Centre in downtown Toronto, and we saw Harry Belafonte. So began a romantic courtship. He took me to shows, bought me jewellery, introduced me to his family, and gave me rides to work. By March 21, I asked Larry to marry me, and five months later, in August 1966, we were married. We're still together today.

Larry is a quiet man. He played violin in a community orchestra, and loves gymnastics. He's politically interested in what's going on, was active in his union local as a secretary and, unlike me, he's not an emotional person. He also has epilepsy. One time I was called by someone from a union meeting, asking me if I knew where Larry was. Turned out he was wrapped around a telephone pole in their parking lot. Because of his epilepsy he averaged a car accident every year for ten years till finally I said no more. He hated not driving but there was no choice. A couple of years later he said he was going to the doctor to try and work out a way to be able to drive again. I told him, "You do that, dear, and you better find another wife while you're out there, because you won't have this one anymore."

He still has the wife and does not drive. I didn't want to look after a dependent person for the unforeseeable future when it could be avoided. Children, I reasoned, would eventually grow and no longer be dependent.

At the office where we met, there was no hint of behaviour from my co-workers that indicated sexual harassment was part of the workplace. We never talked about it, not among my co-workers and not management. There was also no education around it, which could have been helpful for my later experience. As it was, I didn't even know what it was.

Larry was transferred to Hamilton about three months before our wedding day. He was so lonesome in Hamilton he drove to Toronto to see me. At 11:00 p.m., my mother sent him back to Hamilton, not allowing him to stay overnight. On the way he had a car accident and ended up in hospital.

Once we were married, I asked to be transferred to be with my new husband. But to get a transfer to Hamilton, I had to promise my employer not to get pregnant for two years. I didn't do that and my request for the transfer wasn't granted, so I lost my job. I quickly got another in an office in Hamilton, where I worked for three months, until I lost it after a miscarriage. That's the way it was for women in those days (and maybe it hasn't changed a lot in many sectors). There was nothing I could do about it. It wasn't secure or unionized and I'd been there less than three months. So I collected unemployment for a few weeks, and it didn't take me too long before I got a job as a cashier in a fabric store.

In 1968, I had my first baby, a boy. When the baby was three months old, I returned to work part time at the fabric store and worked until my second baby was born, but was never happy with the babysitter. Getting good quality daycare was not possible, either being non-existent or well out of reach financially. I decided I would not have a babysitter for the children until they were old enough to talk, and as it turned out, this is what happened.

Living in Hamilton was worrisome. Apparently, in 1968, Stelco, one of the big steel producers in Hamilton, set a record for steel production. We could see the soot falling all around us. Even on our baby's face. We weren't comfortable raising our children in these conditions.

MOVING TO NORTH BAY

In 1969, and now with two babies, Larry requested a transfer to North Bay so we could live where the air was cleaner. He had lived in Sudbury, in the north of Ontario, before being transferred to Toronto, and it too had its problems with pollution. North Bay was also in Ontario's north, but from what we knew, it didn't have a problem with industrial pollution. Not that we knew it at the time, but one of its biggest industries was the Canadian military, something I would get to know very well.

We settled down to raise our family and, not long after, I was pregnant with my third baby. I always got up with the children over the weekend to be sure that Larry could sleep in. It didn't occur to me till years later that I should have been able to sleep in too. On weekdays, Larry looked after the children from 7:00 p.m. till we went to bed, and I looked after the children if needed during the night. I remember this was when I started to wear socks to bed because I couldn't get back to sleep when my feet were cold.

Having bought a home and with Larry getting a cut in pay transferring to North Bay, a year-and-half after moving, things got tight. We rented out rooms. Two more babies were born in the two-and-half years that followed, and we now had five lovely children. I had always wanted a big family, but for the first few years in North Bay, I also had no friends. I was very lonesome and became depressed because of the isolation and the work of having a lot of babies so close in age. I wanted to pay some bills and teach my children independence. With all these factors, I started to look for a way to make money and get some social contact.

JOB HUNTING

When my youngest was a year old, I started to sell Tupperware. I could arrange it so that most of my away time from home could be done at night after supper when Larry was home with the children. I liked selling Tupperware, meeting new people, and I was good at it. My success, though, caused problems—if you got better than the other sales reps, they didn't like you. There were other problems with the work. At times, I had to travel long distances, say to Sudbury, which was about one hundred and twenty-five kilometres away. And getting paid by the people who bought the Tupperware was hard! I started to see that it cost me more money to have the parties than I could possibly make. I had to buy Tupperware to demonstrate it, and one time had to pay another dealer when she had to do a party for me. I wanted to be paid for the work I did. If I worked ten hours, I wanted to be paid for ten hours. I stopped selling Tupperware when I realized it was not a reliable way to making a living.

I did make friends, though, from my time at Tupperware. It got me out and into the community. I also got another long-lasting good thing from that time. At one of the parties, I got a puppy, named Sam, for the kids. He turned out to be my dog, and he loved me to pieces. When things got very bad, later, I couldn't say for sure that he saved my life, but he definitely saved my sanity.

Meanwhile neighbours had begun asking me to babysit for them. I was already looking after my children, and so it worked well to add another one or two. I took on one child full time and one part time and did this for a couple of years. After that, I worked as a house-keeper at a local motel for six months on weekends, where I was offered the job full time, but declined. The pay was too low to work steady days and pay for childcare. I then got a job as short-order cook in the evenings. I had to convince the restaurant owner, who thought I might have poor attendance because of the children, to hire me. He needn't have worried about that. I held the job for over two years and, except for vacation, I had one Saturday off and a half-day sick, as I recall, all without pay, for a little better than minimum wage. The chef pinched my bum, which I didn't like at all, but I learned to stay away from him, and it didn't threaten my job. The woman I worked with, who had been there for six years, made only fifty cents an hour more than I did. It was a dead-end job, and we worked only the hours we were absolutely needed and then went home. It was hard, hot work.

July 1977, I asked the boss for a raise. When he said I was not good enough for one, I made up my mind to find another job. I wanted to find a job with more of a future, better pay, and steady hours. I went to the Canada Employment Centre where I was advised about more jobs just like the one I had, minimum wage, dead-end jobs. I told them I already had one of those and wasn't interested in trading one dead-end job for another dead-end job.

2

No More Dead-End Jobs

FINALLY, A GOOD JOB

IN 1977, I AGREED TO HAVE MY NAME PUT ON A LIST FOR THE cleaning service at Canadian Forces Base North Bay, in the Department of National Defence. I knew nothing about CFB North Bay or National Defence, but the employment counsellor assured me it would be steady hours and better pay. I had been insistent that I wasn't looking for another low-paying, dead-end job. There were also jobs in the food services at the same place, but she said the pay was lower and didn't recommend it.

So I went ahead and applied to the National Defence cleaning service. It wasn't long before I was called in for an interview and was put on a list to be hired.

As far as I can remember, the interview took place in the Federal Building, downtown North Bay, the same building as the employment office. There were three men asking the questions, such as "Could I mop a floor?" and "Could I use a scrubbing machine?" As I had never mopped an industrial floor or used a scrubbing machine, I lied. I remember very little of the interview and didn't think about it after it was over. By the time I was called, I had even forgotten I had had the interview.

When I did hear from them, they were asking me to come in for a trial of two weeks. But this didn't make any sense to me. I was still working in my other job, and said I wouldn't quit a steady job to go there for two weeks. I was also told I'd be replacing one of the men. This made me kind of nervous, so when I was called again, a few weeks later, to work for four to six weeks, I again said I wanted to work but wouldn't leave a steady job only to go on unemployment insurance after they were finished with me. I was still anxious about the fact I'd be replacing one of the men. When I was called a third time and offered a full-time permanent position, I was told it would be the last offer. I decided I had better take it and said to myself that it was silly to imagine there were only men working there.

I started October 3, 1977. The only time I had been on CFB North Bay before this was when a friend and I went to the base store and she drove. My first day on the job I couldn't find my way off the base at the end of the day and followed a car that got me to a whole other part of North Bay.

I quickly learned it was not silly to imagine only men working there. National Defence had just started to hire women that year, representing a huge change in department policy. They were responding to a recently introduced mandate from the federal government—they had to hire women. It was new ground and I was breaking it.

When entering the base, the base headquarters were on my right. All of the areas where I was to work were within walking distance of each other. I would park my truck in the parking lot for the barrack block where the office of the foreman of cleaning services was located and walk everywhere from there. Foreman is the title that was used then, and, since they were all men, it didn't seem out of place.

Once on the base, the first place I would enter would be barrack block 11 and a bit further was barrack block 13. These were the accommodations for the various military ranks. Across the road was the recreation centre for the enlisted men and women and beside it was the mess for warrant officers and sergeants. Further along was the swimming pool and post office and behind the post office was the fire station. Around the corner was a hospital, quarters for the warrant officers and sergeants, and the recreation centre for the higher-ranking officers.

LEARNING THE ROPES

We were assigned various buildings to clean. I knew how to clean, but it became clear to me that cleaning wasn't the most important thing. The most important thing that we had to do was to sign in and out on time. No one seemed to care what happened in between. The attitude was that if it doesn't get done today there is always tomorrow. This was not the way I was used to working.

In my first week working on the base, I was replacing someone on sick leave for a few days. I was assigned a barrack block for warrant officers and sergeants. This meant changing the sheets on the beds, replacing the towels, and doing whatever else needed to be done. The first unpleasant discovery happened when I opened the cupboard doors where the supplies were stored. They were covered with *Playboy* centrefolds—all of them. I could not avoid seeing them and would have liked to have gone my whole life without seeing these pictures while I worked. It was a shocking beginning to the job. Although it did make me feel very uncomfortable, being new I didn't think I had the right to comment. And it wasn't going to be my regular area of responsibility.

This was a union job and nationally we were organized by the Public Service Alliance of Canada (also known as PSAC) and more locally by a component of it, the Union of National Defence

Employees (UNDE). During the first week I "worked" with the Union of National Defence Employees local president. He was assigned a barrack block that was used as temporary quarters, called the transient block. Our job was to strip the beds and place clean sheets at the end of the beds. These accommodated men (all the accommodation was for men) that did not have high enough rank to have the beds made for them. We were supposed to at least dry mop the floors, and the washrooms had to be clean. Instead, we sat there most of the day drinking coffee. I don't think that there was even three hours of work done in that whole day, and the dust balls were still rolling under the beds when we went home. Some of the other barracks there had mould growing in the showers.

From the beginning, the chain of command for my work was never made clear to me. Supervision was not regular or clear. This made it hard because I never got any feedback as to what was expected of me and whether it was achieved or not. Because of this, I tended to overcompensate to ensure that everything that could possibly be expected of me was done. The problem was that there were not any set guidelines, so I was never sure.

I worked as hard or harder than most of the other cleaners, which caused a set of problems of its own. Some of the men didn't like the women coming in and doing a better job than they did. When I was in an area where the work expected was more clearly defined, there was not enough work to keep me busy. When I found myself with a workload so much lighter than what I was used to, I did more than was expected of me. I had to develop methods of stretching out the time and working more slowly, which was very tiring. When I was with another cleaner, we would talk or I would read or knit.

But I kept at it and things were rolling along fairly nicely. I had a system, but the system was still loose and it was difficult to get any feedback. Supervision still seemed a little lacking, training was limited, and I didn't know whether I was doing what was expected and if they were happy with my work.

I had always been interested in unions, and in December 1977 the Union of National Defence Employees local had their annual meeting with the election of the local executive. I ran and won the position of secretary. The following year I ran for and won second vice-president.

FAMILY LIFE

I now had all my five children, ranging in age from four to nine. The youngest was in daycare, and the other four were in school. I continued working weekends at the restaurant as a short-order cook until December of the year I began at National Defence. My first paycheque from them wouldn't get to me for at least six weeks after I began, and we needed the income.

I worked at the restaurant on Fridays and Saturdays, beginning my shift at 5 p.m. and ending at 9 p.m. or sometimes to 1:00 a.m. At National Defence, I worked weekdays and started work at 7:30 a.m. and finished at 4:00 p.m. For the three months while I was working both jobs, I had to put the evening meal together on Friday in a hurry and then drive the fifteen minutes to the restaurant for work. When I started working at National Defence, I stopped renting out rooms. Before I got used to it, for the first month at National Defence, I would fall asleep when my work was finished. The combination of not being used to my hours and the light workload, sent me to sleep. I never got caught. There was an easy chair behind a door, and even in my sleep I would hear someone before they came into my cleaner's room.

The kids had a key to let themselves into the house, since they were home before me or Larry. There wasn't a lot of home time or family time, except a bit on the weekends. I had planned to spend more time with my youngest son, as he was kind of short changed with one-on-one time with me.

I was still finding life in North Bay very isolating, although by now I had made some friends. I had met my friend Grace when I was having my youngest child, and we stayed in touch for many years. She was very supportive of me later when I needed it the most.

I do remember some good vacations. My husband and I bought a trailer in 1973 and took it and all the kids camping when we had a chance. We did the best we could to give the children a good life.

DENNIS BRENNAN ARRIVES

In April 1978, I received a performance appraisal at National Defence. It was so good that my lead hand, who wrote it and was leaving his job shortly, was told to downgrade it. I was not allowed to keep a copy of it and didn't see it until I got it much later through access to information. In my first few months I received a preliminary assessment, one less formal, which was also good and I was able to take a copy home. I still have that copy.

The first foreman I worked under retired a few months after I started. He was inclined to pinch the women's bums so I had kept away from him, and I knew he would soon be leaving. He didn't pose a threat to my job, and I managed to avoid him. I didn't feel any need to report his behaviour.

The new foreman of cleaning services, Dennis Brennan, became a different story. He arrived in North Bay from Sudbury and started May 1, 1978. He was a burly ex-policeman, and the first week he was on the job he came around to visit each of the staff. When he came to see me, I was in the lounge area of the women's washroom, an area usually off-limits to men. I wasn't comfortable with him from the start. I resented that he was intruding on my lunch break, and I wasn't happy about him coming into the women's washroom lounge. He towered over me at over six feet to my five foot five.

Even though I was initially uncomfortable around Brennan, I got used to the way things worked. I liked my job, the steady hours, and better pay, at one dollar per hour more than my last job. And I received another raise before the year was out. I didn't have to work nearly as hard as I had in my other jobs, and I found I was getting good money for what I did.

COMPETITION FOR LEAD HAND

There were about thirty-nine people altogether in the cleaning services, one foreman, two area foremen, six lead hands, and thirty cleaners. During my first year as a cleaner, I had three levels above me: lead hand, area foreman, and foreman. In September of 1978, a year after I had started as a cleaner, a competition was posted for two positions for lead hand. I was concerned about applying for this position because it meant working one step closer to Brennan, and I was already thinking the less I saw of him the better. However, I reasoned there would still be the area foreman level between us, and since I didn't like the way I was being managed maybe I should do something about it. If I didn't get the job of lead hand, at least I would have tried to make a difference.

Women had not been hired by CFB North Bay in the cleaning services until the previous year, when they were hired for the first time. Of the five women now working as cleaners, I was the only one who applied for the position of lead hand, along with fifteen men, most of whom had more experience and were older than me. I thought to myself, "There is no reason I can't do this." So I ignored my anxiety and went for it.

If I was hired into the new position, I thought there was at least one area I could make a difference. I didn't like not knowing what was expected of me. Changing that would make the job of cleaner easier. I could ensure those who worked under me knew what was expected of them, and I could give them feedback and praise when appropriate, so they would know how they were doing. I could also ensure an effort was made to have their supplies on hand. If the cleaners had doctor's appointments or valid reasons to be away, then all of those things could be taken care of by me. I always liked the feeling of being part of a team and reasoned that as lead hand I could make the cleaner's job better.

I don't know if it was widely known that I had applied for the position. I encouraged another female cleaner to apply, but she wasn't interested. I got a bit of an impression from Brennan that he wasn't happy that I had applied, but nothing specific, until a few days before the interview. Brennan gave me a speech which lasted about an hour. One of the things I remember clearly that he said was that I was too emotional for the job. I was already concerned about getting that one step closer to him, but had convinced myself that with the area fore-man still between us, I could keep my distance.

The day before the interview I went to the office to get cleaning supplies, as was customary. Dennis Brennan was in the office. It had become clear to me for some time that Brennan had mood swings. He had quite a temper and, at least two or three times a week, he would yell and swear at people at the drop of a hat over very petty things.

My practice was to go to the office and get the supplies I needed, but there was no clear set procedure. This is what I normally did and had not encountered a problem until this day. It was hard to know what the correct procedure was and whether or not you were following it. And, say, you did know the rules, often they were changed and, as far as I could tell, there was no standard practice for informing us when this did happen. This unknowing on the part of the cleaners was one of the things I wanted to change if I was successful getting the promotion.

On this day when I went to pick up my supplies, there was nothing unusual, with various people in the office. On a usual day, I would find other staff in the office, cleaners, a foreman and lead hand, or so. I set out to go about my business and collect my supplies. Brennan decided that I would have to go through my lead hand to get my supplies. He lost his temper and yelled and screamed at me. I felt humiliated and ended with a rare headache. I almost didn't go to my interview the next day.

I then had a little talk with myself and analyzed what had happened. I asked the question who was wrong—him yelling or me asking for the supplies the way I did? The answer I came up with was that he was wrong for behaving the way he did. So, I dried my tears and decided to go to the interview after all.

*   *   *

Even before my interview day, I had a sense I was to be treated differently. My interview was scheduled on my day off, and I don't think that was an accident. I think the others had interviews during working time. Even though, at that time, I worked weekends, I also worked some weekdays, and my interview could have been scheduled on one of those days.

There were three people conducting the interview: an area foreman, a military representative, and Dennis Brennan. The interview consisted of a set of questions—a test—posed by the panel of interviewers, and I was to answer to the best of my knowledge. From what

I could tell, when I got the right answer the interviewers would put a tick beside the question. Sometimes I would keep answering till I saw them mark the tick on the paper. They caught on to what I was doing and told me I wasn't to go on a fishing expedition. It was all done in an interview style—that is, someone asked me the question and I said my answer. The questions had been set beforehand by Brennan. The selection of the successful candidates was decided on the basis of how many points each person got for the right answers. I felt good about the interview. Regardless of whether or not I got the job I thought I had done well.

When I later heard that Brennan said that it was the hardest competition he had ever set, I couldn't believe that was the case. I thought to myself, "I am not that smart, but is he really that stupid?" At the time, I thought the questions were not that hard. On the other hand, I hadn't learned most of the information that helped me with the interview from training given by the employer. I had worked hard on my own to get to know my job and had picked up tips from other cleaners. I had heard from one of the cleaners that when washing a wall you start at the bottom and not the top, so I got that right. The work I did with the union was another source of information for me, giving me an advantage. I had already been on a union course where I learned about workers' rights and what the employer could do. I learned what the employer had to do if employees were late and the responsibilities of the employees, such as to phone in if they were off. I forgot about the requirement to fill in the leave form, so I got that wrong.

I was shocked when I later discovered several cleaners thought I had cheated. Major Ryan's notes, which I saw in the court proceedings, said he thought that was the "hammer I held over Brennan's head." In other words, he thought that Brennan had given me the answers and wanted to keep that fact hidden. I also found from court records that I had an almost perfect score on the interview.

At least a month later, those of us who had applied received a sealed envelope, which was customary in competitions for a job! When I received my envelope, I didn't open it. I went to pick up the youngest child and spent at least an hour at the babysitter's place. Still I didn't open the envelope. I waited till I got home and opened it with Larry.

I had won the competition for one of the two placements, behind an ex-military man who got extra points for having been in the armed forces. I was excited and felt good about my accomplishment. I had won the competition! I understand that ex-military members no longer get extra points in competitions for these positions. The next day, when I went to work, the kitchen staff were happy for me. That did not last long.

PROMOTED

After waiting for the three-week appeal period, I started the new job as lead hand on November 20, 1978. My instruction sheet had only a few lines describing my duties and used only the male gender. There were many ways the few female cleaners working at National Defence were made to feel as intruders or invisible, and this felt like just another one of those. At this point, I was more nervous than excited about the job. I had worked there a year, and this was a big step.

It took only a day after I started for the resentment that my staff and supervisors had for me to surface. The men resented that I was their supervisor and gave me the cold shoulder. I didn't have any women to supervise.

Just as Dennis Brennan used the chain of command when it suited him, my area foreman also ignored the hierarchy. He would directly instruct my cleaners, who in turn would not inform me either accurately or in a timely way what the area foreman had already told them to do.

On November 21, I was supervising a worker in the warrant officers and sergeants' mess. His task was to clean the kitchen staff's washrooms. I will never know whether it was stubbornness or laziness but, whatever it was, he didn't want to do the work. It was my job to follow up to ensure his work was done. That same day, Brennan had spoken to me, saying that the foreman for this area was not doing his work. Later that day, the area foreman told me not to check this particular cleaner's area more than once per day. He also told me to bend more. I said I would bend more if the cleaner did his work. I was in a no-win situation: if the area was not clean, I would be responsible, but when I insisted on the work being done properly, I was told I was not doing my job right and to stay away.

I went to see another cleaner in the recreation centre, an area I supervised. He didn't like me coming around or me being his boss. When I asked him some questions about the area, he got angry and told me to "get the hell out of the building." I said that I would go when I decided to do so. I asked the area foreman for support but got none. Worse than that, he said I should apologize to the cleaner who had yelled at me. I refused to do this.

On November 25, 1978, the area foreman apologized to me for the way he spoke to me on the preceding day regarding some comments he made about Brennan.

On the twenty-eighth, I had to speak to the area foreman about a cleaner's work. I had seen the cleaner standing at the bar smoking and had yet to see him do any work that afternoon. Later that day I was told by my area foreman to lay a charge against the worker who told me to "get the hell out of the building." This didn't seem like a good idea. This was the same area foreman who earlier had not supported me, and now he was advising me to lay a charge. I couldn't make sense of it.

Brennan was absent during this time, and he had encouraged me to go to the major responsible for cleaning services if I had any problems. So I decided to ask for an appointment. On the twenty-ninth, I went to see the major. My conversation with him centred on the fact that both the cleaners and the area foreman were causing me problems by changing agreed-to instructions. My supervisor would send a cleaner to one area and not inform me of the changes. This led to misunderstandings and frustration on the part of the cleaners and of me and undermined my position as the supervisor. The major listened to me, didn't offer any solutions, and took no action. In the end, I just felt embarrassed and never went back to see him again, that I recall. I felt any attempt to speak to him would be a waste of time.

It was around this time that my area foreman asked me to resign my position in the union because I was a lead hand. He had no right to do this, but I also believe that he didn't want me to attend the steward's course coming up soon, which would give me more knowledge of my rights on the job. He was right to be worried. The courses were empowering, and it was there I met Marie McNeely, who would become instrumental in my eventual support network.

On the twenty-ninth, after Brennan's return, he told me that he would discipline the cleaner who had yelled at me, but I don't believe it was ever done. At this stage, though, I believed he was helping me to succeed.

Another incident occurred just before a meeting I had to attend when the area foreman told me to find a cleaner who was supposedly at the recreation centre. This was on a cold and blowing winter day in January. It was a large base and there was some distance to walk. I found the cleaner somewhere else—it turned out to be where the area foreman had actually told him to be. It took at least half-an-hour longer than it should have to find the cleaner, and I was late for the meeting. I had a feeling I had just been set up.

This kind of sabotage was going on all the time in varying degrees. I was trying to get a vacuum repaired. I couldn't fix it myself and had to go through the area foreman. It took weeks of follow-up before it was finally working, and it was my responsibility to keep the floors vacuumed. Meanwhile, I had to vacuum with a poorly working machine.

I took it a day at a time and decided it could only get better as the men got used to me being their boss. It should have worked out. If management had backed me, I'm sure it would have.

3
The Harassment

THIS CHAPTER WAS THE HARDEST TO LIVE AND THE HARDEST TO revisit to write. It was long ago now and a nightmare. Many friends and people I respect have urged me to write this book. My eventual standing up for myself resulted in the changing of the law. I am proud of that. But it began here. At the lowest point in my life. Without understanding this part of the story, none of the rest makes sense. My hope is that my story will contribute to understanding what sexual harassment at work feels like from the inside.

Many more people now are sharing their stories of sexual harassment than they were in 1979. But even now, I seldom if ever hear them describe exactly what happened. They say it was awful. But I don't think you can know what that means until a few of us share some of the details.

I wrote a lot of this chapter thirty years ago. When I revisited it for this book, I was embarrassed. I felt awful all over again. I am told that the transcripts of the Canadian Human Rights Tribunal are worse. I don't have to go there. This is hard enough.

I want people to understand what it is like to be under attack at a workplace. How unwanted attention, beginning as an annoyance, can relentlessly escalate to the point that it dominates your life. People talk about an imbalance of power. But what does that mean? What does it feel like to have your boss—who has the say over whether or not you have a job—weekly, daily, hourly, even calling you at home, harassing and demanding attention from you. What does it feel like to live in this bubble, where no one else apparently sees what is happening to you, and you are too afraid to tell anyone, and all along you imagine that you can take care of it.

I didn't understand it could get so bad when it started. I did know that what was happening to me was wrong and that I wasn't making it happen. But it took what felt like a long time for me to ask for help. (Although, when I look back now, and see that it can take much longer than it took me, I think maybe it was fast.) And after I asked for help it took a much longer time for the people in power to listen. (No wonder some people never speak out!)

Dennis Brennan was trying to get me to "consent" to being raped by him. This idea occurred to me very quickly, and it still feels like a good description of what was happening. This may sound confusing, to twist the meaning of consent like this, but this is what Brennan was doing. He was twisting meanings. Even at this early stage, although I wasn't aware of what it meant to be "groomed" by a sexual harasser, I was aware that what Brennan was looking for was not an equal human exchange. He was seeking to coerce me into doing something I didn't want to do—in a twisted way to get me to "consent" to being raped. He wasn't "making love" to me. He was harassing me.

SLOWLY, SLOWLY, BIT BY BIT

January 2, 1979, Dennis Brennan told me that he would train me on the projector that was used for the training films (this was before videos!). Although nothing inappropriate happened during the time, I was not comfortable. The two of us would be alone in a darkened room. I think I felt uncomfortable or suspicious because I was the last of the six lead hands hired and none of them had been asked to do this. In retrospect, I now realize that Dennis Brennan had already started to sexually harass me, although at the time I didn't realize it.

Already, he would frequently summon me to his office. I usually didn't know when or why, only that I had to go since he was my boss. He also called me at home on my days off. One time, on my day off, he called me at 7:00 a.m. to find out why I wasn't at work. Not only was it not his job to call me, even if I had been supposed to be at work, but I didn't start at 7:00 a.m. My shift began at 7:30! He constantly bypassed the chain of command, and I felt that I was being very closely and oddly scrutinized.

The days of my shifts changed frequently, sometimes starting at 6:00 a.m. or 7:30 a.m. I often worked on the weekends and after March 16 I was always put on weekends. Brennan would change my days off from Thursday and Friday to Wednesday and Thursday, so he could be sure to see me before he went off for the weekend.

He also came in once around six in the morning to supposedly supervise work that I absolutely did not need help with. His usual time for coming in was 8:00 a.m. It should have been my area foreman supervising me, if anyone had to do it. He came in some Saturday mornings, too. Brennan also made it a habit to place me so far from my area foreman that I would be forced to rely on him, Brennan, for instructions and work support. At the same time that he would isolate me from the area foreman, he would also start a disagreement with the area foreman. I was supposed to follow the area foreman's instructions, but now I had conflicting instructions. So the thing was, whose instructions do I follow? I knew it had to be Brennan's because he was the boss.

Brennan shared an office with the two area foremen, and he insisted that several of the staff eat lunch in the office. I was always the only woman, and there were usually two or three lead hands there. Usually the discussion centred around dirty jokes. I don't think I heard any as filthy before or since. Brennan was the instigator of most of them and told the dirtiest ones by far. It got to the point where I refused to join them for lunch despite repeated requests by Brennan. As a local union executive, I had access to a different room, and there was also another room where people signed in and out, which is where I would often go for lunch breaks to read. At one point, I was told I was not allowed to read on my breaks because the military would think that I was sloughing off. I didn't stop because I knew that what I did on my breaks was my business.

One day while I was present, Brennan called the area foreman into the office for some small reason and humiliated him in front of me. It appeared very deliberate and was an example of the intimidation that would keep me from reporting him as his harassment escalated. Brennan would always make it very clear what would happen to someone who crossed him, and I sensed he also wanted to be very sure that I knew this and saw examples of his power. It crossed my mind to wonder if my turn to be humiliated was next. Other times, I thought what I was witnessing could have been set up as an act between the two of them, because they also appeared to be great buddies.

Almost daily, Dennis Brennan would ask me how I was and all about my family. He would go out of his way to seem friendly and supportive. I felt there was something funny about it, but I dismissed my gut instincts. I now know that this constantly singling me out and making me the object of his comments and attention was the beginning of the harassment, and an escalation of harassment is apparently typical grooming behaviour. I was being groomed.

WHAT'S WRONG WITH HIM?

On Friday afternoon, March 16, 1979, in an isolated cleaning service office in barrack block 11, Dennis Brennan, with his fully erect penis exposed to me, said "How would you like a piece of tail?"

My very first thought was *What's wrong with him?* I mean, I couldn't make sense of what was happening. When the pieces of the scene in front of me started to fit back together (and this is all happening fast inside my head), my next thought was *I may as well kiss this job goodbye*, immediately followed by *I'm not quitting. I guess I'll have to push through what is to follow to keep my job.*

Out loud I said, "Thanks but no thanks."

I was shocked that he would show me his penis and suggest I have intercourse with him. In my head, I had two options: quit, or deal with what was happening as best I could until my probation was over, which was May 20, two months away. I figured as long as I was on probation, Brennan held the power. Once I passed probation, if Brennan didn't leave me alone, I could complain. I liked the work I was doing, and I thought that in time my staff would accept me as their supervisor. I had just done a lot of reading on assertiveness and was working hard at it. I knew I had the right to say no, and my reading was giving me ways to do it. And why should I quit? If anything, Brennan should go if he couldn't keep his hands and his penis to himself.

I stayed.

I think if this had begun when I first started as lead hand, I may have just stepped down and gone back to the regular cleaner's position, realizing this was too much to battle. At this point, though, after four months of hard work learning a new job and struggling the whole way with all the male staff, I had already invested a lot into it. I was sure I was good in the position and could do a good job. I was too close to completing my six-month probation to walk away. And I thought I could handle it. I mean, we were adults. If he had some kind of problem, well, he should fix it. It wasn't me with the problem.

So began a very intense struggle. The last two months of probation I can only describe as living a horror story and nightmare. It was far more difficult to get through day-to-day than I realized, and I coped far less well than I anticipated. Nothing in my world to date had prepared me for this. I had led such a sheltered life. I had never even heard some of the terms he used to talk about sex and was not entirely sure what he was implying at times. This man just would not accept that I wasn't interested in a sexual relationship, and he kept the pressure on.

The following week I went on a supervisor's course in Brockville and tried to put what happened out of my mind. But it was constantly there, in the back of my brain. Maybe, I thought, he would drop the pursuit. That didn't happen. When I returned, I came back to an intensified assault of verbal abuse from Brennan and a barrage of personal questions concerning my sex life. I didn't know what to do or say. When do I need to engage because he's my boss? When can I tell him it's none of his business?

Brennan made every opportunity to get me alone with him, and then he'd begin with the questions, each time more intimate. When I did answer, he'd throw my answers back at me, commenting, for example, on how deprived I was for not having had sex with men other than my husband. This would be followed by a suggestion (or demand, depending on his mood) that I should have sex with him. I refused sex with him so many times, I couldn't guess how often. I never treated it as a joke, and I never joked with him. It was just too scary. He said I had an emotional hang up because I would not give myself permission to have sex with him because I was married. He would make all of this appear to be normal conversation, like it was my problem if I got upset instead of going along with him, as if it were normal for a boss to speak to an employee like this. Brennan spent a great deal of time and effort to get me acquainted with crude sex terms. He would explain different ways to have sex. He'd tell me I was a prude for not having sex with him. I had never dealt with a boss on such a personal level before, and it was confusing and alarming.

I did not know how far Brennan would go, but I felt I needed to deal with this on my own. I felt like I *should* be able to deal with this on my own. And I had a job to do, which I could do very well. I had already gone through far too much to give up my job. I believed there was no option for me but to hang in there and cope until my probation was over or his abuse of me stopped. And, I reasoned, why wouldn't he stop when he realized that I wasn't going to agree to have sex with him?

Brennan demanded my presence in the office to such an extent during the month of April and part of May that I was only out in the base working something like five hours a day. I couldn't get all my work done in this time so he reduced the amount of work I had to do. His pattern or method of operation was to have me in the office, on the pretence of work, an average of half an hour to two hours a day. This was extremely emotionally exhausting. During this time, when I was scheduled to be in the office with him, was when he bombarded me with sex questions and proposals. His moods went up and down, and my emotions were twisted and turned. After particularly difficult times, I'd leave his presence and double down on my determination to manage on my own. I was sure that as long as I was on probation, I couldn't bring in a third party. Thinking back, I realize how little I knew about the behaviour of harassers.

Brennan's grooming behaviour was an escalation from the bum pinching that I and my fellow women workers had silently tolerated and, mostly, managed to avoid. We just got on with work. Bum pinching was an open secret that we, as women, had been (and often still are) expected to manage on our own. "Being a woman had required a lifetime of ignoring such insults," as Monica Hesse characterizes American Congresswoman Alexandria Ocasio-Cortez's words in Ocasio-Cortez's July 2020 response in Congress to a publicly uttered sexist insult by a fellow Congressional Representative. Ocasio-Cortez goes on to say that "when you do that to any woman. . .[you] give permission to other men to do that," and she was "here to stand up to say that is not acceptable."

Brennan knew that no one of his male colleagues was going to tell him that his behaviour was unacceptable. And my job was to carry on, to get the work done. I did not yet have the knowledge to recognize that what he was doing was typical sexual harassment behaviour and beyond anything I could manage on my own. Today, even with the strength of my own victories, I feel supported when I hear publicly spoken messages like those expressed by Congresswoman Ocasio-Cortez and learn about informed sex education at home and in schools. These give me some hope that other women and girls will have the tools to recognize sexual harassment earlier than I did and maybe they will be supported when they do.

Meanwhile, I was doing what I knew how to do, and that was to carry on, to get the job done. To manage on my own.

Brennan, I had learned over the past ten months, was a person with a big ego. On several occasions I told him that I was not interested in forming anything other than a work relationship. The harder I tried the worse it got. I kept telling myself that so far it had been just talk, nothing had happened. I was wrong, of course. Not only had he exposed himself to me, but by taking out his penis he was aggressively harassing me on many levels.

On Friday, April 6, Brennan detained me after my shift on the pretext of work, something he had started to do very frequently. He quickly changed the subject to sex talk and asked me several times if I wanted to have a "piece of tail" with him that same afternoon in one of the bedrooms of barrack block 11. I kept telling him I didn't want to go. He persisted. I kept refusing. Finally, I was nearly in tears, so he said I could go home.

I went home, going over and over in my head ways I could get out of this. Things I could say, things I thought I *should* have said, that would stop him. That would finally convince him that I wasn't interested. That all I wanted to do was my job. I wanted to work, and go home and be with my family. I was so upset and I convinced myself that if only I said the right thing, he would stop. I had to stop it now. I felt that during office hours I was not able to speak freely. Work hours were for work talk—even if Brennan didn't follow that rule, I still felt restricted by it.

I had access to Brennan's phone number, through a base phonebook with military members' and civilian employees' phone numbers and home addresses. Both Brennan's and my phone numbers and addresses were in it, so I phoned Brennan at his home, desperate to end the situation. I arranged to meet him at the office that night at 7:00 p.m., with the intention of finally getting him to drop his pursuit of me. Now.

In the dry language of the Court of Appeal, the decision states that "in hindsight," I was "ill-advised ever to telephone [Brennan] or to visit him after hours to reason with him." I did not have the wisdom of hindsight. I had my own council and my experience of successfully managing everything else in my life, up till now. I did the best I could. How do I explain—how does anyone explain decisions made under stress?

My morale was very low and I didn't realize how vulnerable I was. Of course I didn't succeed in persuading him to leave me alone. Instead he coerced me into masturbating, which he offered to do for me, and put his finger in my vagina.

UNDER ATTACK

I didn't want his attention and I couldn't get away from it. There was not a moment when I was at work that I wasn't thinking about how to keep away from him. How to put him off. How to keep my job. How to get to May 20. I never knew what to expect next. I had a right to the job and I needed it. Each encounter with Brennan left me angrier, and I would convince myself that I should be able to stop him. That I could cope. On various occasions Brennan would hug me, sometimes touch my breasts, ask if he could kiss them. I never let him. I count that as a victory.

After a while, each time we were alone in his office, he had me put a dinner knife in the doorjamb—I'm not even sure, now, what the purpose of this was. Most other times the door to his office would be open. No one ever came to the door when I was there with Brennan. Brennan said that the knife was there to alert him if anyone was coming in the door. He also said that it was a warning to others not to come in. Even though the office belonged to Brennan and the two area foremen, it seemed to me it was Brennan's office, and he let the area foremen use it at his pleasure. I also believe that they both had an idea of what he was doing. Whatever, it was offensive to me that I had to lock myself in his office.

Every exchange with him could turn bad. Sometimes I would manage to discourage him—maybe he would sense that I was near a breaking point—and he would say that he would leave me alone. But he never did.

Looking back, I wonder how I stood up to him at all. I wonder at my own strength. But at the time, all I could think about was how to keep one step ahead of him, how many more weeks were left, and could I keep going.

Against my will (and certainly it was not necessary for my work, in fact, it made my work that much harder), Brennan was arranging my working hours so that I was required to spend more and more time in his company. He was constantly probing into very personal areas. I was on edge all the time. He would ask me all kinds of questions about my background: Where had I worked in the past? Where did I meet my husband? Once I admitted to having had problems with my nerves four years earlier and that I needed to take medication for about six months. He then asked if I had any of that medication left and asked me to give him some of it. I did one time, but when he asked for more I told him to see his doctor. I would give in on one thing to him and then stand up to him on the next thing. His probing was intense and invasive. Finally, I couldn't take any more, my anxiety was so high. I asked to be on leave for the week of April 9 to 12. It had been at least five years since I remembered taking a week off on leave.

But this didn't stop him. Brennan just phoned me at home.

Brennan's talk about sex went everywhere. He was talking as if it was just a matter of time before I would agree to have sex with him—"consent" to be raped by him. As I was to learn, this is a known strategy of escalation of sexual harassment. Rape was next.

At some point he started to brag that he had had a vasectomy so he could have sex and not get any of the women pregnant. This gave me an idea of how to put him off. Larry and I had decided not to have any more children, and Larry had had a vasectomy. So, around the third week of April, I suggested it was too bad Brennan had a vasectomy. I thought I could maybe trick him into stopping his pursuit by telling him I wanted to have another baby. Quite a gamble for me! But inside the bubble Brennan had created around us, this made sense. My job, I felt, was to convince him that he didn't want to have sex with me. To make him stop, to open his eyes to the error of his ways. And inside this backward world, this new and desperate strategy seemed reasonable.

It didn't take long to find out he did not have a vasectomy. Where he got the idea to say he had, I have no idea about, but I called his bluff. I bought some time. My raising the idea that I *wanted* to get pregnant made him nervous. In this Brennan bubble, I had scored. Maybe he hadn't ever seriously considered the idea that if he did succeed in having sex with me, I could become pregnant. The sex talk didn't stop, but for a while it centred on the risk of getting me pregnant. My apparent willingness to have another child seemed to bother him.

I was on days off that week but he still phoned me at home as often as he felt like. He arranged for me to meet him in front of Mike's Milk, a local convenience store, at 2:00 p.m. He said if I did get pregnant that I would "squeal" sooner or later. He also said he wouldn't be able to bear to see me at work knowing it was his baby. He said it would worry him too much. He then suggested I go on the pill. I told him that was impossible, which is when he said I should go to the drugstore and look for other means of contraception. Inside the Brennan bubble, there was lots of this type of talk.

Maybe it was this conversation or maybe it was another, but I was recognizing that I wasn't coping, and I was making a bad situation worse. My efforts to outsmart and outmanoeuvre him by engaging him enough to keep him from physically attacking me or reporting me for insubordination were not working. I didn't yet know enough to realize that Brennan was holding all the power that mattered, and there was no way out for me. My husband, Larry, who I had not yet told, knew there was something wrong. I was in a rough state emotionally, crying a lot at home, yelling at the kids, going to bed late and sleeping poorly, having nightmares about work. I was taking extra showers. I figured if I did not go to sleep, I would not have to get up in the morning (no logic there). I was finding it hard to cook meals. I'm sure Larry didn't suspect anything with Brennan, but he did tell me I'd better get things straightened out at work since that seemed to be the source of the problem.

So I persuaded myself, again, that I could end this. That I could convince Brennan to leave me alone. That I wanted nothing personal to do with him. I had had enough small victories over him that I thought that I had a chance to get him to finally believe me when I said no. I never felt free to say what I wanted to say at work—he was the boss. So, I phoned Brennan at his home and arranged to meet him at the North Bay Mall, at 7:00 p.m., the night of April 11. I again tried to get him to stop, to get him to leave me alone. Again, I told him that I wanted no part in any relationship.

At this point, I just kept telling myself to keep going. That I could manage. I was trying to make sense of a situation that made no sense. As much as I could believe when I was away from Brennan that I could reason with him, that I had every right to my job and to be left alone, when I was in the Brennan bubble, the reality of his presence took over. He was over six feet and two hundred pounds to my one hundred forty pounds. I feared his mental stability and his quick temper. When he was angry he was scary.

I drove a GMC Suburban, which I referred to as my truck. The North Bay Mall parking lot was right across the street from Brennan's apartment building, where I had once worked as a housekeeper. When I arrived, he came to my truck. I immediately stated my case. His response was to take his penis out and ask me to give him a blowjob. He said he wanted to be sure I knew what I was missing. He was aggressive and persisted, not to be denied, saying things like "I bet you didn't know they came that big?" referring to his penis. Knowing how fragile his big ego was and afraid that he would physically hurt me, I decided it was the lesser of two evils and did what he asked.

I was making one of those calculations—if I do this, then I can avoid that. If I allow this bad thing to happen, then I can avoid that even worse thing. This is the kind of calculation that many of us do, often referred to as choosing the lesser of two evils. But when both "choices" harm you, and you would not choose to do either, then this is not a choice.

Each time after I found myself forced into making one of these impossible "choices," I would review what had happened and vow that it wouldn't happen again. I would build myself up to be strong again, going over in my mind what else I could possibly do to stop him. I kept looking ahead to my goal of finishing the probationary period, when I thought I would finally have some power in the situation.

I had a little over one month to go. Looking back over that time is so painful. I am not a weak person—maybe if I were, I wonder, would Brennan have left me alone? My strength both helped me and it hurt me (but in the end, my strength saved me and I'm proud of that). My strength of character kept me going, but that doesn't mean I wasn't hurt and hurting. I wasn't sleeping. My life at home was awful. The longer I kept all this to myself, the harder it was to turn to someone for help. Somehow, I still believed the problem would go away. And why tell anyone? If I didn't say anything and Brennan stopped, it would mean I had handled it on my own. I even thought about writing notes about what was happening. I just *knew* that what Brennan was doing was so wrong, and I guess in my mind I had the idea, even then, that someday he would be held accountable. But where would I hide these notes to be sure no one would see them? In the end, I didn't keep notes, at least not as it was happening. But I have a good memory and eventually was able to write what happened by connecting the dates and events with other things happening at the same time.

I also didn't know who to turn to if I did decide to speak to someone. I had a close friend in North Bay, but it was a bad time to visit. North Bay is on the shore of Lake Nipissing, and it was the spring flood season. Everyone was on edge as we watched the waters rise and wondered how high it would get this year. She was the only one I could think of to tell.

As the idea of telling someone grew in my mind and the probationary period came closer to ending, Brennan's onslaught intensified. I would attempt to get Brennan to leave me alone by reasoning with him and trying to talk my way out of any further sexual pursuit. He would take my attempts as encouragement and keep pressuring me to have sex with him. It was never ending. The sex talk. The constant pressure.

One of his tactics was to corner me in a cleaner's room and close the door, or he would order me to pull the curtains closed in the union office and then try to hug me and have me touch him. When I refused, he accused me of being mean and selfish for not meeting his demands or agreeing with his moral standards. He would look at me as though I had no clothes on, leering. When I met him in his office and he had me put a knife in the doorjamb and demand that I close the curtains, I never did this without him first telling me to do so, even though I knew he would demand it. I made it clear that this was not my choice.

I WAS LOSING WEIGHT

On April 27, during my lunch break, I asked Brennan for the afternoon off on sick leave. I was tired and run down. I had been sleeping badly and not eating properly for several weeks since returning from my course in Brockville in March. He suggested that I go and rest in one of the barracks, and he would be in to see me later. This wasn't what I wanted, but I desperately needed to lie down. I went and rested for about an hour and a half. He came to see me at about 2:15 p.m. He said he could see I was not going to give him a "piece of tail," but with the door closed behind him, he took his penis out in the cleaner's room saying he wanted me to give him a blowjob. He had asked me several times since April 6 whether I wanted him to masturbate me. He complained that I never asked for a "finger-wave," as he called it. Since that first time, on April 6, I was successful in never allowing him to ever touch me there again. I figured if I felt him up at least he would not touch me.

Again, that calculation—if I do this, then I can avoid that, the thing that is even worse. Each time it feels like a minor victory, until later when it just feels bad. And I couldn't sleep or eat properly.

Early the following week he gave me heck for not arranging to see him more. He was always having to call me in the office or detain me. I told him I was trying to get rid of his sexual attentions not build on them. Still, he kept having me put a dinner knife in the doorjamb as some sort of signal. He complained when I didn't always close the curtains as he asked. Each time, it was a little victory.

His constant comments and demands were not only sexual. He chipped away at my self-esteem and confidence. At my character. At my defences. By early May he began telling me that I would fall flat on my face without his support as my foreman.

He always had some reason to contact me. Around the first Thursday of May, when I had Wednesdays and Thursdays off, at about 9:15 a.m., shortly before the union management meeting at base head-quarters was to begin, he phoned me at home to complain about the meeting. First, he gave me heck for reminding two other people to ask permission to leave as they were scheduled to attend the union management meeting. He was going to refuse them permission to leave. I told him I was still going because it was on my own time and that I would be the only union member there. I said I was also prepared to let the rest of the committee know why the others could not be there.

He continued with his game of give and take. He changed his mind and said it was okay—he would let the others go to attend the union management meeting. But this meant I should go to see his apartment. He often talked about his apartment and what he had there. So I went to his apartment and nothing happened. He met me at my truck and brought me to the back entrance and accompanied me up to his apartment, which from what I saw, had nothing special in it—just furniture. He showed me around and talked for about five minutes. Then we both left. I had to be at the base by 10:30 for the union management meeting. That was it.

With less than three weeks to go till my probation was up, I was so close and still felt at risk. One time, when he had me in his office for no good reason, I was sitting there thinking *Why am I sitting here? Get up and leave!* And so I did. I got up to leave, at which point he threatened that if I left the office before he said I could go, he would charge me with insubordination. I didn't think I could get away with it, but I am glad I tried.

He had frequently tried to get me to be away from home on a regular basis, so my husband would not notice it as something unusual. It was not something I was about to do or ever did. I never went away from home on a regular basis. I would not have done that even if I had the time. I was always on edge, looking out for the next trap. I just kept postponing what he wanted. I was exhausted, but the end was getting closer. I don't know if something happened to scare him off or if I was getting used to it, but for those last three weeks things seemed to be slacking off a little.

MY PROBATION ENDS

Finally, the paper came stating that my permanent position would come through. At this, Brennan said I still had thirteen days to go, because the paper work for my job went in late. I did not believe him and said so. This thing I had worked so hard for was going to happen. I should have been ready to celebrate. I should have felt good. Instead, Brennan was right there, making the case that it was all his doing. He asked if I would give him a big kiss. I refused. I said the most he would get from me was a big smile. He never gave me anything except trouble. What I got I had earned, and I was not giving him anything.

On May 22, just before Brennan was due to go on holidays, he asked me to come to the office at about 3:00 p.m. He wanted to show me a method of having sex in the office. I had refused to rent a motel room. I had refused to have sex in my truck or to go to a drive-in, and on and on.

I planned it so I did not get to the office till about 3:20. He gave me heck. He would hardly have enough time to get an erection, he said. Meanwhile, I was in survival mode, something I was practised at by now. Brennan, though, wasn't giving up. He didn't want this to be a waste of time, he said. He grabbed me and lifted me up on the desk in the union office and took out his penis. He tried to kiss me and show me how he intended to "screw me." He wanted to get me to feel him up so he would get an erection, but I was not cooperative, so he tried to give himself an erection. But he was having trouble. He was too aware that the cleaner was in the hall. He couldn't "keep it up." I convinced Brennan that sex with me was not possible because my husband would find out for sure. I told Brennan I could not keep it a secret and Larry would be sure something was wrong. I finally managed to get away.

I am convinced to this day, if he thought he could have gotten away with it, he would have raped me that afternoon.

After about ten minutes, he left the union office and went back to the cleaning services office. At about 3:45 p.m. my husband phoned to remind me that today was the federal election and not to miss voting. Remember, during this entire period I had not told anyone what was happening. My nerves were a wreck. I thought I was coping but knew I couldn't for much longer.

This was the end. I was sure beyond all doubt that Brennan would stop at nothing till he had raped me. I was sure beyond all doubt that there was no way I could resolve what was happening without bringing in a third party. I was now at the point where I didn't even dare to risk that I could any longer put him off. The longer I stayed silent, the heavier the burden had become.

There had been times when I considered jumping off a cliff. When I couldn't sleep and, after a humiliating confrontation with Brennan, these were the thoughts that came to me. But I wasn't going to do that. I said to myself that nobody *but nobody* was going to cheat me out of seeing my children grow up. They were at the ages of six to eleven and still had a lot of growing to do. To be honest, I wasn't thinking about them. I never even thought what it would be like for them growing up without a mother. It was me and my right to see them grow up that I was thinking of. Selfish as that was, it was the right thing to keep me alive.

This left me only one option. It was time to complain. Brennan wanted me to "consent" to being raped. I wasn't going to do that.

I believe that from the time he showed me his erect penis he wanted to rape me, but with the twist that he would use the power of his position as my boss to convince me to go along, essentially, to give me permission. I'm not saying he was looking for a "consensual relationship." I'm saying that after two gruelling months of Brennan's harassment, of him using his power as my boss to wear me down, to break my will, that if I had not been able stop him, and he had raped me, it wouldn't have mattered what words I had said that may have implied consent, it still would have been rape.

When just before his vacation he physically lifted me on the desk, that was the turning point for me. I saw three options: 1) go to a third party; 2) be raped; or 3) quit quietly. Each had serious consequences. I was in a lose–lose situation.

And I knew I would lose my job anyway as Brennan would find a way to have me fired.

The third option was not something I wanted to do, either. I would have to find another job, and there were few good jobs in North Bay I would qualify for with my education of high school.

I took the first option, not knowing where it would lead.

From the time Brennan had exposed himself to me, it had been ten long weeks of constant physical and psychological harassment, and I had reached my limit.

4

Speaking Out and Backlash

I BROKE MY SILENCE ON MAY 24, 1979, FOUR DAYS AFTER THE END of my probation. I knew Brennan was about to leave to go on summer holidays. The longer I kept this to myself the harder it had become to say anything and the greater the burden grew inside me for not speaking out.

I began by briefly telling my family doctor what happened. From there I found the courage to tell Larry, my husband, that same day. Now that I had opened my mouth, I decided I wasn't going to shut it. Thankfully, Larry was very supportive and did whatever he could to help. He immediately put me in touch with a counsellor where he worked and made an appointment for me to see him later that same day. Larry was not angry with me, but he was very angry with management on the base. It was such a relief to have Larry's love and support and to not be dealing with the harassment alone anymore.

Back to work on Friday, May 25, I mustered up every shred of courage I had. It helped that at last my probation was over, but had it not been over, I still would have gone ahead. I could not have tolerated this pressure for sex any longer. When Brennan called me into the office that morning, I made up my mind to tell him as clearly as I could that there was nothing on earth that would convince me that I would in any way tolerate his sexual advances any longer. He said it was a mean thing for me to say just before he was going on holidays. I said it was the best time to tell him. I said he would go and have a good time, and when he came back he would know that he would have to leave me alone.

Brennan was in Saturday, May 26, at 7:00 a.m., and had me in the office till 8:15 a.m., wanting to know if I had changed my mind and reminding me that it was a mean thing of me to do. The rest of the talk was general. I refused to talk about sex and knew that he was scheduled to be away for four weeks. I also knew that after he returned, I would only be working for a few days before I would go on my own holidays for three weeks. I believed it was possible that this time Brennan would hear me, and with the holiday break this might bring an end to the harassment.

But I didn't stop there. I guess by now, the reality of the past few months was sinking in. In late May, just after Brennan went on holiday, I prepared a brief statement saying that I had been sexually harassed by him. I took the statement with me to work. I hadn't decided exactly what I was going to do with it. That day, I had the statement with me as I was speaking to the union steward. I was looking out of his window as we spoke and I saw a union official from Labour and Trades go by. For whatever reason, at this moment, I decided I would give the statement to him. I caught up with him and provided him with my brief statement about Brennan's sexual harassment, signed and dated. I made him aware of what was happening, but I asked him to keep it in confidence. I still had the hope that Brennan would stop, and if he did I wanted the option to keep it quiet. I was scared. I had confronted Brennan, and now there was a third person in the workplace who knew. It was no longer just Brennan and me. In my mind, even now, I was trying to fix the situation. Speaking to the union official from Labour and Trades was a step forward, truly outside the Brennan bubble. I kept those steps going forward.

If Brennan stopped pressuring me for sex, I wanted to drop the whole thing. I never intended to make a formal complaint. I simply wanted some protection in case Brennan made an attempt to get rid of me when he realized that he could not continue. Knowing I had Brennan's four-week holiday absence and then my following vacation a few days after his return, it was such a relief. Working without him around was healing and gave me the strength to stay.

* * *

Bonnie and Larry Robichaud family portrait, 1979. This photo was often used by the press when covering Bonnie's case.

Brennan returned to the base on June 18, a week early. This was a shock. I was expecting another week of work without him, before I went on my own holiday. I was working the day he returned but managed to put off going near his office until the afternoon. By about 1:30, I could put it off no longer. My shift ended at 2:15, and I had to see the area foreman. When I walked in, Brennan told the two area foremen to leave and shut the door behind them. He kept me there about fifteen minutes, again making sexual advances. I raised my voice and made it clear that I had not changed my mind and was going to inform a third party. (What I didn't know, was that by this point, Brennan probably already knew about my complaint.) He told me to leave the office. As I left, he added that it looked like I had gained weight and asked how things were with my husband. I left the office feeling angry and frustrated, humiliated, and powerless. I felt like laughing or screaming or crying. I didn't know which. All the strength and confidence I had gained in his three-week absence was evaporating.

There were people standing in the hall as I walked out. I found my voice and made an oath, out loud: "Whatever it takes under the sun, he will never, ever do that to me again." They looked at me oddly, but I didn't care. I kept my oath that I made that day, but I had no idea that there would be *so much* under the sun.

I vowed Brennan would never again look at me as if I had no clothes on, or ask me if I was horny, or ever again invade my privacy by asking personal questions he had no right to ask.

He was there for only that one day and I was shaken up, but nevertheless, I finished the week at work. This time, I went to the union steward and told him that I wanted to now make my complaint formal. He told me to write up a "To Whom It May Concern" letter, and he would bring it to P.G. Howe, the base commander. I did this, dated June 22, 1979. Somehow this letter never officially reached the commander.

Now that I had decided enough was enough, making a formal complaint seemed to be my only option. I was still plagued by thoughts of jumping off that cliff. Doing something about the situation was the only way to silence them.

I also wrote up the complaint and gave it to the union official from Labour and Trades to let him know what was happening.

In the meantime, I was very scared to be alone with Brennan. My shift started early the next morning. I bought my husband a meal ticket to join me for lunch, for which I was subsequently reprimanded, apparently not being allowed to bring my husband to the officers' mess. I had called Larry that morning to come and just be there in case Brennan showed up. Brennan did not.

This was the beginning of my long struggle forward—the complaint procedure with the union, the presentation of grievances, my complaint to management, the Public Service Commission, Workers' Compensation Board, the Canadian Human Rights Commission, and the grievance hearings. I had no idea of all the twists and turns that lay ahead.

BACKLASH

It's impossible for me to be sure, but judging by the events that followed Brennan's unexpected return from holiday, it seems likely that when I told the Labour and Trades union official about my experiences and asked him to keep the information confidential—he betrayed my confidence.

In the week that Brennan unexpectedly returned, I was away for a few days for French language assessment in Toronto. As part of my new position, I was required to have an AA level of French. When I was back in North Bay, on my day off, I was ordered in to work by the union steward, who wouldn't say why. I said I didn't want to go in on my day off, but he said I had to. He told me to go to base headquarters. I had no idea why I was being ordered in—I thought maybe it was something to do with the letter I gave to the Labour and Trades union official about the sexual harassment. It was not.

Upon arrival, Captain Adlard, who was the military representative for civilian staff, told me to go to the cleaning services office. There I was asked to wait with Brennan and an area foreman. We waited for forty-five minutes, during which time I did not speak. Brennan and the area foreman then walked me to headquarters. On the way over, Brennan walked on the outside, because, he explained, "You are not for sale." As far as I can tell, Brennan seemed to believe that he was protecting me from being mistaken for a prostitute by having me walk on the inside, away from the street's edge. I found the whole performance and its implications insulting, but I didn't have the stamina to make a scene.

I still had not been told why I had been summoned. Finally, I was led into a meeting with Captain Adlard and Brennan. It wasn't until the meeting was well under way that I realized this was a disciplinary meeting and I was the one being disciplined! I was told that there was a petition with sixteen signatures asking that I be relieved of my duties, "so that more favourable attitudes may once again be restored among the workers." I was also told there were fourteen letters of complaint written against me, all within three days, the three days, coincidentally, since Brennan had returned.

I was completely unprepared. Here, I had thought my employer may be responding to my complaints of sexual harassment, and instead, I am being confronted by complaints about my work, in the presence of the harasser. Once I realized what was happening, I had to almost interrupt Adlard to ask to see him alone or to have a union representative with me, but he refused my request. So, with Brennan right there, I told Adlard I had been sexually harassed by Brennan, and I tried to explain that my complaint about the incidents of sexual harassment might have been the motivation for this campaign against me. I somehow had the presence of mind to note that all the letters and the petitions were done within three days of each other—the Monday, Tuesday, and Wednesday after the Friday that I signed and dated the "To Whom It May Concern" letter—and I pointed this out to Adlard, and asked if that didn't seem suspicious to him. Brennan jumped up and down out of his chair and threatened to sue me.

Captain Adlard's response was, "Whatever relationship you had is now over; this is just between the three of us and nobody else needs to know. It does not have to get to suing." He added that he was just coming out of a divorce and that he did not want to deal with this kind of thing, as if that had any relevance to this work situation.

(Another odd detail is that I was summoned to this meeting by the union, in fact, by the person in the union that I had given the "To Whom It May Concern letter," and not by management. None of this made me comfortable or seemed right.)

I was not soothed by his words, so Adlard told me I could take the matter to civil court. I told him, "It happened at work, and it will darn well be fixed at work."

The next day I was handed a "Memorandum of Shortcomings" from base management dated June 29, 1979, stating that although my "work as a cleaner has been most satisfactory . . . a very high percentage of the cleaning staff have seen fit to indicate their dissatisfaction [of my supervision] in writing." I was still to be a lead hand but with reduced personnel to supervise. My authority as a supervisor had been taken away.

No attempt was made to even acknowledge my concerns, let alone address them. I felt like a steel door had been slammed in my face. I now felt even more frightened and afraid to speak and did not feel safe from being sued by Brennan. I realized *I* was the one perceived as the problem.

This meeting made it clear that there would be no support from management in solving my complaint against Brennan. My long-awaited vacation was coming up, but I didn't want to go away with this hanging over my head. I tried to postpone it, thinking it could be solved before I left, but my request for a change of leave was denied. Imagine how naive I was, to think that it could be solved so quickly!

I spent the first few days of our camping holiday pretending I was chopping Brennan's head off when I was chopping wood. Wood chopping wasn't usually my job. Normally, Larry would have done it. Next, I played nursery rhymes over and over on the eight-track tape player and sang along with them, until Larry made me stop. After that, every night at the campfire, Larry and I would spend hours trying to figure out how we were going to fight. It was not a restful vacation.

* * *

My first day, after my vacation, I wrote a three-page memo in answer to the memorandum of June 29, but I didn't send it to Captain Adlard. I felt it would make no difference, and it was embarrassing. In it I had explained what Brennan was doing to me.

In the days following my return near the end of July 1979, although I still received the pay of a lead hand, I didn't have the duties. I felt devastated by the demotion. I loved my job and thought I was a good supervisor. I was subsequently isolated, disciplined, and given a heavy workload. These were extremely difficult times for me with bouts of crying and severe depression. Just making meals at home became a very difficult task. The nightmares I had experienced during the harassment did not stop and I was sleeping poorly.

Isolation was the hardest of the difficulties I was experiencing. On my first day back to work after the sexual harassment complaint, I went for a coffee break at the cafeteria on base. Many of us had a coffee break at the same time, and I was a few minutes late arriving. When I walked in, everyone got up and walked out. Brennan, who almost never came to break in the cafeteria, was there and so were the two area foremen. When Brennan left, every one followed him out. I was shocked; I had never experienced anything like that before.

The shunning kept happening for several days. Then I was told I was not allowed to go to break in the cafeteria anymore. I challenged this by submitting a grievance and was again permitted to take breaks in the cafeteria. But the shunning continued, and everyone still kept leaving when I arrived. Sooner or later, I thought, they would get tired of missing their breaks, but after several weeks of this, the ones who liked me least just stopped coming. After a while it was too much, and I occasionally took my break alone in my cleaner's room.

This awful treatment was hard to bear. My depression deepened. No one would talk to me. I felt as though I was always being watched. The effect of this type of shunning was devastating, but I wasn't going to be defeated. I knew I had done nothing wrong. At one point, I bought a book on body language. I thought if I could not talk to anyone, at least I wanted to show that I was strong by walking tall and sitting straight and looking confident. In reality, I was scared all the time. I don't know if this strategy had any effect on those around me but I felt stronger as a result.

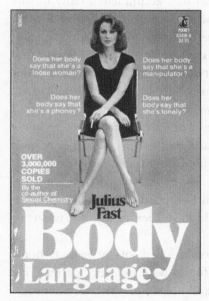

The copy of *Body Language*, by Julius Fast, that Bonnie bought in 1979. Book purchases were uncommon in the Robichaud household, as the family budget was tight, and this was considered an essential purchase.

I was assigned a barrack block to clean, referred to as the punishment block. I had gone from supervising five cleaners to one very uncooperative half-time person. I used to comment that I never knew which half I supervised. Hard as it had become, it was still better than the sexual harassment and staying silent.

Only three days after I had been assigned to the punishment block, my supervisor found some dead flies on the windowsill and claimed they had been dead and lying there for three weeks.

It was the time of year that dead flies accumulated daily on the windowsills, attracted by the heat and the sun. A good friend of mine suggested I find out if it was possible to determine how long the flies had been dead. I phoned the health department in North Bay to find out how long it took for rigor mortis to set in. It took three calls; luckily no one hung up on me. I was told once rigor mortis had set in there was no way of knowing how long the flies had been dead. I was sure there was no way my supervisor had the resources to know either. Besides anything else, as far as I remember it, I had only been assigned this block for three days when this happened, so even if his charge was correct, how these three-week-old fly corpses were my responsibility, I'll never know. When I stopped to think about it, the accusation was so outrageous it could have been funny, if it wasn't so serious.

Despite the extreme stress at work, I had lots of help at home with Larry, who was behind me all the way and very patient. He helped prepare meals with the kids and helped me with all the tasks I had related to moving my complaints forward. And of course, he was also working at his own paying job.

GRIEVANCE PROCESS

Marie McNeely, the union representative I had met at the union course in Kingston in January 1979, was already becoming an important support for me and would remain so. With her encouragement, I decided to officially submit grievances to my union. This is a completely separate process from the "To Whom It May Concern" letter I had submitted earlier. To follow the proper procedure, I was to go to the union steward, and it was their job to write up grievances or at least help me to do it. They know the rules about which forms to fill out, who gets what, and the timelines. I met with him to begin the process of drawing up the grievances, a process that seemed to drag on and on. I felt that the grievances were not getting written. He had meetings with management, without me, and I felt that he was stalling the writing and presenting of them.

Usually, the grievance process begins with the writing up of the grievance, assisted by the union steward, who then gathers the signatures and submits it. Before submitting it, the grievance is signed by the griever, a union official such as the steward, and a representative of the employer. The first two levels take place at the local level, and if the grievance is not resolved, it goes on to the third level, which is regional, and then the fourth level is the national office. At each level, there is an opportunity for a hearing, a reply, and a resolution. When a resolution is not found, it can be transmitted to the next level. Each level also has set timelines that must be followed.

Although it was only a week after my return from my vacation, it felt like forever, and I had the distinct feeling that I was being given the runaround. I was definitely feeling stressed and sensitive, but the union officials who were meant to be helping me seemed to be deliberately trivializing my complaint. "Yours isn't the only complaint," "These things take time," and so on.

"A Guy Had the Right to Chase a Woman"

During a meeting, the union official from Labour and Trades informed me that his personal view was "a guy had the right to chase a woman if he wanted to." My stress level was not reduced! Even though he was not the person in the union that would be likely to represent me, he was meant to support me. I also didn't trust the union steward, whose job it was to represent me, but who I felt was putting me off. Neither had given me any indication that they would stand up for me to management. I couldn't trust them to write up and hand in the grievances.

* * *

I was so frustrated I called Marie in Kingston and spoke with her for an hour, crying almost the entire time. I was a basket case. But not so much that we didn't get work done during that phone call.

We discussed formulating the grievances and came up with ten of them. After the call, I typed them up myself. One of the ten was not accepted by the union steward—it had to do with allowing employees time off to get names on a petition against me. I could let this one go. The nine that were eventually accepted by the steward were as follows:

1. I grieve my employer's decision to withhold letters of complaint against me. Corrective action requested: That I get a copy of each letter of complaint.
2. I grieve my employer's decision to withhold a copy of a petition signed against me as a supervisor. Corrective action requested: That a copy of the petition be given me.
3. I grieve my employer's decision to not go through proper procedures with regards to written complaints against me.

Corrective action requested: that I be allowed to settle with my employer's cooperation each and every complaint.

4. I grieve my employer's decision to unjustly order me to work on my second day of rest. Corrective action requested: that this practice be discontinued, a written apology be given me, and that all material pertaining to this matter be removed from the files and destroyed in my presence.

5. I grieve that my employer did not follow proper procedures in the memorandum of shortcomings dated 29 Jun 79. Corrective action requested: that all copies of the memorandum of shortcomings be removed from my file and destroyed in my presence.

6. I grieve my employer's decision to restrict the number of employees I supervise to less than those in my job specifications. Corrective action requested: that I be reinstated to my former status as lead hand as was the case prior to 28 Jun 79.

7. I grieve my employer's lack of proper supervision. Corrective action requested: I request formal instruction on proper supervision.

8. I grieve my employer's decision to allow sexual discrimination on the job by my foreman. Corrective action requested: That every effort be made to eliminate sexual discrimination on the job. That my foreman be appropriately disciplined for allowing sexual discrimination on the job.

9. I grieve my employer's decision to decide that sexual harassment on the job by my foreman is strictly a matter between me and my foreman. Corrective action requested: That my employer stop the sexual harassment by my foreman.

After I typed them up, I took the grievances to my union steward, who signed these nine. With these nine signed grievances in hand, I arranged to have them signed by management, which as far as I knew meant Brennan.

Brennan had to sign them as received, and I could only get his signature on my own time, meaning, on my coffee break. He read them as he signed them and laughed and made them appear trivial and acted as if this was of no importance to him. He used the excuse of the austerity program, which was in effect at the time, to keep the carbon paper for use at a later time—as if to show me that the only value in the grievances was the non-reusable carbon paper. There were six copies made, one for him.

Whatever he was up to, there was no mechanism for him to circumvent the process now that I had my signed copies. I had made up my mind to fight back, and I made a formal complaint. There was an obligation in the collective agreement that once a grievance was presented and signed it had to be actioned.

GRIEVANCES HEARING—LEVEL ONE

The wheels had started turning. I received a letter from the union telling me that I would be required for the grievance hearing, at base headquarters, on Tuesday, August 7, 1979. This was only one week after I had submitted my list of signed grievances. Now, suddenly, everything was moving fast. I was asked if the hearing could be recorded and I agreed, as long as I received a copy. The only person opposed to the taping was the union steward. I was told that because it was such a sensitive topic they would question Brennan separately. I was expecting him to be there and had psyched myself up for it. I insisted that Brennan not receive a copy of the tape of my side prior to his evidence.

The hearing was poorly organized and rushed. There was not

nearly enough time scheduled. No break was planned, and there were no glasses of water at the table. Two hours into it, I requested a break. I needed to go to the washroom. On my return, they discovered they had another meeting scheduled, and half an hour later I was told to wrap up. I was not finished speaking. The most important questions around sexual harassment and discrimination—the last two griev-ances—had been left to the end and had not been adequately dealt with before we ran out of time.

I returned to work the same day of the hearing, feeling drained and disheartened. Within an hour or so after the hearing, Brennan stormed into my building and started yelling at me, saying the place "looked like hell" and to clean it up. I felt physically cornered by him. I was already stressed after the long hearing, and he was acting like a crazy man and using abusive language. I was afraid and called the steward, who called Captain Adlard to come and inspect the build-ing. In the end, Adlard finally found some dust on top of one of the partitions of the third-floor washroom. As a result of the frivolous accusation, Brennan was not allowed to supervise me for six weeks. A small comfort. This was a setback for Brennan, but he was still my boss.

I got the grievance reply later on a Friday just before the weekend, after a full week of work.

There is a pattern here, which is to make it difficult for complain-ants to get proper rest and to recover. At the grievance hearing where I spoke, I was told that they agreed not to give Brennan a copy before his hearing, but when I received his copy, it was clear he had read what I said and so he had access to mine before his hearing. Brennan's hearing was two days after mine, on August 9.

I lost everything at the first-level grievance. Everything was dismissed by National Defence. As was evident in the reply to the first-level grievance, there was no understanding of what I was up against or of the situation of someone in my position. For example, the reply to grievances 8 and 9, dated August 10: "Why did Mrs. Robichaud feel that she had to tolerate this kind of behaviour during her period of probation knowing full well that any supervisor or individual found guilty of this kind of behaviour would be subject to immediate dismissal?"

I transmitted all nine grievances to the second level.

5

Setting Boundaries

ABOUT TWO WEEKS BEFORE THE SECOND-LEVEL HEARING FOR my grievances, I was relieved to receive the local president's permission to have Marie McNeely come from Kingston to be present at my hearing. Even at this early stage, and with little experience of the process I would come to understand so well, I had learned how important it was to have support. About five days before the hearing, I was home with work-related stress, and Marie called me to say that the local president had just told her she wasn't allowed to attend after all.

I didn't know where the pressure had come from but I was livid at the power of the union steward, to go back on his word and leave me without the support I knew I could receive only from Marie. This decision and an article I read in the newspaper about sexual harassment motivated me to write a letter to the Ontario Human Rights Commission. This started a whole new set of wheels turning. The Ontario Human Rights Commission directed me to the Public Service Commission Anti-Discrimination Directorate, since I was employed by the federal government. When I learned of this, I got the Anti-Discrimination Directorate's address and contact, and by early September 1979, I had submitted a complaint letter to them with a number of enclosures.

I was then told by the union steward that the base commander had given in and was going to give me what I asked for in my grievances. This was supposedly why I would not need Marie there to support me.

GRIEVANCES HEARING—LEVEL TWO

Three days before the second-level grievance hearing took place, the decision to not allow Marie to attend was overturned, and once again I was told the union would allow me her support. I was never given an explanation for the steward's change of mind. Nor did I tell him that I had mailed my complaint to the Ontario Human Rights Commission. By now, I had lost confidence that this complaint was going to be solved on the base alone.

The second-level grievance hearing was held on September 11. In answer to grievances 1 and 2, I was finally allowed to see the petitions and letters of complaint against me. It was at this point I realized only three cleaners had complained about me in writing. Although, in the written response to the grievances, they somehow had come up with the number twenty! It turned out, there was a second petition with additional names. The first petition had only the names of men, while the second included some women's names. Five of the letters were from Brennan, one from a lead hand, and the rest from the two area foremen. I later learned some of the names on the petition were people on sick leave, and they were not people who had ever worked for me. And I was told not to talk about the petitions with anyone who had signed them.

The corrective action I had requested for both these grievances was to see them and to be given a copy of them. During the hearing, it was suggested that the corrective action I requested was to see them and then have them destroyed in front of me. This was not my request, and although I became confused as to what my request was, I realized immediately that this was not what I wanted to be done. Colonel P.G. Howe, the base commander, wanted to tear up the petitions and letters there and then. As an aside, I told Marie I didn't want them torn up because I no longer felt my issues would be resolved here at the local union level, and that we may need the petitions and letters later.

Colonel Howe said I had no choice because it was the corrective action I had requested on the grievances. I had requested that the Memorandum of Shortcomings be removed from my file and destroyed in front of me, which may have been why I became confused into thinking that I had requested the same for these. Whatever, I was being told that this was the preferred corrective action and that I needed to agree to it. I hesitated for ten minutes, but in the end Colonel Howe tore them in three pieces and put them on the side table. I later commented to Marie that this didn't look like destruction to me, but she said that was how they did it. (It turned out I was right, and eighteen months later they would rematerialize!)

As a result of the second-level grievance hearing, grievances 1 to 7 were answered. Grievances 8 ("I grieve my employer's decision to allow sexual discrimination on the job by my foreman") and 9 ("I grieve my employers decision to decide that sexual harassment on the job by my foreman is strictly a matter between me and my foreman") were still not addressed and, as time would tell, would not be dealt with for a very long time.

I went back to work, and Brennan and two area foremen came to me in a very small cleaner's room and, I'm assuming with the plan of intimidating me, said, "This is a whole new card game." And I thought *he* wasn't playing with a full deck!

After the hearing I went home crying, yelling, and stamping my feet in frustration. I was glad that at least I now had more staff to supervise, and I was to be moved out of the punishment block, with some measure of my previous position restored. But I was finding the pressure hard to take, and there was still a long way to go before I was going to see any resolution of the underlying reasons for grieving in the first place.

Brennan had been taken out of the chain of command after the first-level grievance hearing. After the answer on September 14, he was reinstated and was once again my boss.

It was after receiving the first-level grievance reply to grievances 8 and 9 that the seeds were sown for pursuing a proper solution to the sexual harassment I received and for addressing management's resolve not to take any responsibility for it. They were clearly not going to do anything about my grievances unless I proved Brennan's wrongdoing.

I knew things would get more difficult now. Management had been forced to restore my authority over my full staff, after I had grieved the cutback of supervision to only one person half time.

After making my complaint of sexual harassment and discrimination, I was not expecting the endurance test that would follow. I don't know where I found the strength to get through it, but I think my experience as a young mother with five small children all at home helped. Anyone who has done everything it takes to get small children through those first years, often isolated from friends and family, knows the stamina, perseverance, and willpower it takes. You can't give up. You fight not to lose yourself or your children. I think this is what prepared me.

COLONEL'S ADVICE TO ME

I received the response to the grievances, dated September 17, 1979, signed by Colonel P.G. Howe. I was considering transmitting the grievances to the third level, and before I had decided what to do, I was called to a meeting with the base commander. Tuesday, September 25, I met with Colonel Howe, with Major Ryan in silent attendance. Before the meeting started, I moved my chair so as to be closer to Colonel Howe's desk and sat down. He then moved to the sofa and put distance between us.

I was not permitted to make notes during the meeting, but I made them right after it was over. I believe his main motivation for the talk was to convince me not to transmit any grievances to the third level. He was giving me a word of advice and telling me he had done what he could to rectify the situation. I had the distinct sense that he believed me—he just didn't believe that going ahead with this complaint was useful for me or for National Defence. He had advice for me and he believed he knew better than I did what was good for me. Colonel Howe said there were still "scars of the old wounds," but the "scars were healing" and I would have to "bend" with management. People were going to be sensitive, and it was best for me not to overreact to the way things were going and not to expect changes overnight.

I explained to him I had no problem with the people I supervised. That was never my problem. My problem was with the people who supervised me, who contradicted my instructions to the point where I could no longer cope effectively. He shrugged that one off. The base commander said he understood I had been given a new area to work in and was assuming some new responsibilities.

Colonel Howe said, "You have got to be careful not to be too sensitive. Don't expect to be treated in a different way; you are going to be treated just like everyone else. You will be treated with the same respect as any other lead hand, and you are not going to get any more, and you are not going to get any less." He also discussed it as a win and lose situation, saying that I cannot just count my wins and losses.

I agreed with him on this part. I wasn't looking to score points. I was looking for a resolution. I agreed that if I started thinking in terms of a win or lose situation, no one wins. If someone loses, everyone loses. All I was asking for was that the grievances be satisfied.

He told me not to make a big issue out of it. He also explained to me how the burden of responsibility for correcting this situation was on my shoulders. I remember this distinctly.

Allowing Discrimination

For my part, I listened to all he had to say, then I started going into it. I said I was happy with the responses to grievances 1 to 7, and pleased with all the effort he put into resolving them. I told him I understood I probably took a great deal of his time and didn't want the effort to go unnoticed, but I did want to talk about grievances 8 and 9. I explained as far as grievance 8 was concerned, in my opinion, allowing an employee to discriminate against someone shows you don't have proper discipline. So I explained that I was not grieving discrimination on the part of my foreman, I was grieving the *allowing* of it.

Colonel Howe had not allowed witnesses at the second-level hearing, and said he didn't understand how it would help to take the grievances to a third-level hearing, because I would not have any witnesses there either. He referred to Brennan and me as two children playing. When one child hits the other child, "Who are you going to believe?" I didn't like the example he chose, but answered, "What if you have ten other children to substantiate that this in fact did happen?" Howe insisted it couldn't be proven; I said it could, but the forum for having proof given by witnesses was denied me.

The Colonel said, "I will not have people coming in here and having witnesses, and I will not play judge and jury over the situation." I explained again the reason I was not happy with the response to grievance 8 was that Brennan was not disciplined. Colonel Howe's response was, "I spoke to him and I can assure you it won't happen again." I told Colonel Howe I didn't think that was appropriate discipline.

I was also not happy with the wording of the answer to grievance 9, "If in fact, sexual harassment did take place . . ." I said that did not sit very well with me. He said, "Now that is going to have to continue to not be sitting very well with you. You are just going to have to get used to it and learn to live with it."

I felt very strongly I did *not* want to learn to live with it and said, "I suffered a great deal and my family suffered a great deal all because of the discrimination by this individual. There cannot be one set of rules for one group of people and another set of rules for another and have things 'work out.'" I said, "right before I go on holidays I get this whooped at me."

I wasn't willing to let things stand as they were. I kept stressing that I received all kinds of disciplinary actions, and Brennan just got "spoken to." I had experienced (and was still experiencing) stress and frustration and had already spent a lot of money and put in hours of work just to get back what I should have had in the first place. At that point, my focus was not about the money, although I did say that I wanted it to be dealt with as well.

Colonel Howe kept telling me this was all water under the bridge. I believe at this point he just wanted me to forgive, forget, and start a new page.

I also described some of the hurtful harassment I had to put up with—harassment *allowed* by management—things like people getting up and leaving the table when I came for a coffee break. I told him I was able to see this for what it was, but I'm also not made of stone. And then there were the actions that affected my working conditions—like, what about the weeks I hardly saw my area foreman, and he wouldn't help me with dealing with my supervision issues? It's part of my job to go through him. It got to the point that I was writing him notes, and he still never responded.

I said I believed in unions and the support they could give workers. I didn't challenge these injustices just for the paycheque. I was happy with my paycheque. So I told Colonel Howe, "I want to know that your officers will know how to deal appropriately with this kind of situation if it happens in the future and not in the same way I was being treated."

Colonel Howe repeated that he thought Captain Adlard could not have dealt with it any other way. I said I didn't agree. Captain Adlard could have saved me a lot of suffering and addressed things from a different angle. Something could have been done at the time to deal with the problem instead of just covering it over and leaving me to cope as I did.

"Educate Us"

"Well, just between you and me," said Colonel Howe, "if it's education you want, there is a one-day labour management course that travels from base to base." He said that he would speak to someone about incorporating my case without names and places so that they could better educate "our people." "Taking this to the third-level of grievance will not achieve anything near what it's going to achieve if you leave it at the second level and instead use this course to educate people," he said. He ended with, "Just take my word for it."

Colonel Howe said if I wished to take my grievances to the third level that was my prerogative to do so, and he couldn't stop me. He said he didn't think I was going to gain anything because I didn't have any witnesses, and he just didn't know what it would solve. He asked me to decide, saying, "You can't get it any better than to put an education system through." I liked the idea. It was what I wanted, and, on the surface, it sounded good. I said I wanted to sleep on it before making my final decision.

I told him I would let him know by Friday, September 28, which was also my time limit for the transmittal to the third-level grievance. Colonel Howe asked me to come and see him either way, no matter what I decided.

After sleeping on it, I decided *not* to transmit grievances 8 and 9, but would transmit some others. I did try to contact Colonel Howe when I had made my decision, but he could not be reached. I couldn't find the transmittal forms at the local, regional, or personnel office and didn't know enough to try the national office. I had one copied, and then no one would sign the transmittal form to send the grievances to the next level. Marie McNeely sent me six signed copies by special delivery. I was going to transmit four grievances (numbers 4 through 7), since theoretically three had been won. I was not going to transmit the ones on discrimination and harassment. So I arranged to have the major sign them as received.

DETERMINATION TRIPLED

A couple of days later, I reconsidered. Brennan said he was going to have me demoted. I think this was October 4, 1979. I was angry. It didn't make sense to still have Brennan as my boss. Without grievances 8 and 9, there would be no resolution. I went home (my shift ended at 2:15), and later in the day I went back to the base and had grievances 8 and 9 transmitted to the third level. I was in reality a couple of days late to transmit them, but they were accepted anyway. I don't know if they ever noticed I was late, but I decided it was their problem if they hadn't noticed.

When Brennan wrote to personnel to have me removed from my job, I put in a further grievance. I thought that Brennan's action would substantiate what I was saying and something would have to be done to alleviate the problem. I have since learned, and it has been the experience of others, that management's level of tolerance of harassment and harassers is incredibly high. The steward refused to sign the next grievance, so I spoke to the Union of National Defence Employees national office, who helped me word the grievance and I signed it.

Since I felt that I wasn't getting good support from my union, in October, the Public Service Alliance of Canada's national office suggested I have a meeting with the staff of Union of National Defence Employees (my union), and that this meeting should take place at the regional office of the Public Service Alliance.

This didn't go very well either, from my standpoint. The meeting was interrupted several times and, other than me, there were only men in the room. I felt stupid by myself, crying and going through all of this alone. I felt torn. I needed to get support and to tell my story, but because of Brennan's threat that he would sue me for slander, I was also now nervous about how much I could safely say.

It was very personal to speak to them about being sexually harassed. It felt voyeuristic. There I was, the only woman in a room surrounded by men, giving intimate details of very traumatic events, with no support. It was awkward, embarrassing, and intimidating, and I felt my complaint was not being taken seriously. On top of that, the organization of the meeting was terrible. It was being taped, which I didn't have a problem with, but the tapes could only hold fifteen minutes each. Every fifteen minutes, I would be interrupted as they changed tapes. It bothered me that the best they could do was tape my complaint on fifteen-minute tapes, as if they had expected my presentation to be less than fifteen minutes. Eventually I just said I was leaving. I didn't feel supported by my local, regional, or national officers of the union at this meeting.

By the end of October, I started French language training for nine months. I think management thought I might forget all about my complaints after being away from my job for so long and distracting me with learning French.

But I was now determined more than ever to solve things.

At the same time that the union process was unfolding, so was the process for the complaint of sexual harassment I'd submitted to the Public Service Anti-Discrimination Directorate.

The Public Service Commission sent an investigator to North Bay. Her main concern appeared to be that Brennan could sue me for slander if I submitted my complaint. Even though this was a concern for me, I said I was not going worry the rest of my life about something that may or may not happen. I had decided that if he didn't sue me, I had nothing to worry about, and if he did—I would deal with it. I had to stop her from trying to intimidate me with Brennan's threats, and I had to get her off that track or she was not going to investigate. (The lawyers always used the word "slander" with me when talking about Brennan's suit, and it was only much later that I learned that both libel and slander are forms of defamation. Slander is mostly spoken and libel is written, published, recorded, and so on.)

The investigator wanted me to write a paragraph on each incident of sexual harassment, so, on December 11, I submitted a five-page report, typed single-spaced on eight-and-a-half-by-fourteen-inch legal paper, plus several attachments, which had taken me considerable effort because of the nature of the incidents. She wanted more information, so I wrote a three-page letter a few days later and said that was all she was getting. It was wearing me out. I was at language training during the time, and I didn't want to risk being dropped from the course and sent back to work because I was failing.

Her report and its conclusion, which took a month to produce, was that my complaint would have to be submitted to the Canadian Human Rights Tribunal.

THERE WAS NO ROAD MAP

I didn't even know what the word "tribunal" meant and had to look it up in the dictionary. A tribunal is similar to a court of law, but less formal, among other things, and hears cases relating to discrimination and other legal inquiries. I didn't understand the process that was starting to take place. I only knew this was the next step. There was no road map. I just knew this would give me an opportunity to have the truth told to a third party. I *did* know that my complaint would be testing the Human Rights Act, but it was the option presented to me and I proceeded.

The more everyone was trying to stop me standing up for myself, the more determined I became. My local union rep tried to prevent me from submitting grievances, Captain Adlard wouldn't support me and wanted my complaint of sexual harassment to just stay between us, Base Commander Colonel Howe tried to dissuade me from submitting grievances to the third level, Brennan was trying to demote me and attempting to isolate me from my co-workers, and the Public Service Commission investigator was trying to intimidate me from submitting my complaint through fear that I might be sued.

I was beginning to think there was something powerful happening here when so many people were determined to stop me. The truth was they didn't believe me, or didn't want to believe me. Or if they did believe me, they didn't perceive it as a problem to solve, more that it was only my problem. I became the problem. If I just went away, so would the problem and nobody would have to actually address any underlying assumptions about discrimination and attitudes toward women that probably led to the sexual harassment in the first place.

I felt I was up against a mountain.

I had put in a Workers' Compensation claim through National Defence in September, to cover the time I had taken off due to work-related stress. Although it was his role to do so, Brennan didn't submit it, so I had to do it myself. In the end my claim was turned down. I had also written to my member of parliament, Jean-Jacques Blais, to explain my situation. He responded twice, once in October 1979, to say it looked like I had the support of my union representative throughout the process and that my grievances were being processed in the normal manner; then in November, asking to let him know if I felt he may be of assistance in the future, in response to a letter from me.

I was getting a lot of push-back and not much in the way of support.

Nothing I had attempted so far had brought me any closer to my goals of workplace accountability and education on issues of discrimination and harassment. At this point in time, I was left with a "Memorandum of Shortcomings" on my file, the letters of complaint and petitions against me (although, I had supposedly witnessed their destruction during the second-level grievance hearing), and multiple threats of discipline from Brennan on an ongoing basis. I still had to be around Brennan on a daily basis.

The worst part of it all was that, to my knowledge, Brennan had not been disciplined for his behaviour.

I felt like I was fighting this alone, and that my life had been turned upside down in a way I could never have anticipated. I was still unaware of the bigger and far-reaching problem of sexual harassment. When a high-ranking military officer on base had told me that I was the only one this ever happened to, I had said that meant it should be easy enough to fix. At the same time, he also asked me if I wanted to be a pioneer. I was confused by what he meant.

With every step I took to resolve what had happened, I felt I was further penalized. I was very angry about the way I was being treated. I was certain that I was not the party who had done wrong. Brennan had done me wrong, the local union had done me wrong, and the employer had done me wrong. Their mutual goal was that I not put in my complaint.

At every turn, I encountered resistance. I didn't yet know what I was fighting.

6
Making Waves: Human Rights Tribunal

O N JANUARY 26, 1980, MY COMPLAINT ALLEGING SEXUAL HARASS-
ment, discrimination, and intimidation by Dennis Brennan and
the Department of National Defence was submitted by me to the
Canadian Human Rights Commission. My best friend in North Bay
signed it as witness. Mine was the first complaint of sexual harassment
to be referred for inquiry by a Canadian Human Rights Commission
since their inception in 1977.

As the pressure against me got stronger, so did my determination
to see it through. I knew I was not the one who had behaved badly, yet
I was the only one being punished.

I was still on French language training, which I definitely needed.
Before beginning this program, I didn't know what *soup de jour* meant.
I couldn't count to ten in French. I had to work hard and focus. If I
didn't keep up, I would have been sent back to base.

Finally, the French language training ended in June 1980. I had
passed. The very day I went back to work there was a day of protest
organized by Brennan. He had allowed staff to object to my return by
taking the day off at the expense of National Defence. About three
quarters of the cleaners stayed away. (Those who didn't have any paid
leave left to use, he gave them the day off with pay.) The protest didn't
work. I still returned to my job. It seemed a somewhat futile gesture if

it was intended to humiliate or intimidate me as I didn't even find out that it had happened until a week later.

REASSIGNED TO CLEAN THE SCHOOL

After returning to work in September, I was assigned to clean the school at CFB North Bay. The principal made a point of telling me she thought Brennan was a real gentleman, and that he would never do anything such as I was alleging. Having a female boss was no guarantee of solidarity—an important lesson for me to learn. Once again, I was subjected to humiliating behaviour.

At the school there were all kinds of petty roadblocks put in my path, from not providing heavy-duty garbage bags for the large garbage pails when requested to withholding the tanks that contain the cleaning solution for the scrubbing machines. The final straw—one of my cleaners changed the desks around in a room for which I took responsibility, which would usually be an action resulting in the cleaner being disciplined. But because the room was my responsibility, he was not disciplined. As a result, I was no longer allowed to clean at the school. The school's principal was never happy to have me there, and I was glad to be moved and get away from yet another stressful situation. On top of that, the evening shift from 4 p.m. to 12 a.m. had been hard on my family life.

Management put me back on the base proper once I left the school, responsible for cleaning a barrack block and supervising a staff of three. Throughout this time, there was a list of places I was not allowed to clean because my security clearance had not yet come in. These included the hospital, headquarters, and the post office, all places I had previously worked when they were short of people. I still had to supervise others who did work in these out-of-bounds places.

Back at the barracks, some of the men I was supervising had been in the competition for the position of lead hand with me, and none had ever been supervised by a woman. Most resented being told what to do by me. Many took advantage of the situation I was in to get out of doing the work they were paid to do, undermining my position as lead hand. As a supervisor, I had always taken the approach of backing my staff, but I was being put into an impossible situation by the area foreman. He would tell me to ask my cleaner to do one thing after already telling the same cleaner to do another at a different location. When I questioned the cleaners on why they were at the changed location, the contradictory instruction became evident. This kind of thing happened repeatedly. It was confusing for the cleaners as well as for me. Who should they listen to—me or the area foreman? It must also have made them question my competency as lead hand. Even so, there were some who were supportive and understood what was happening.

HUMAN RIGHTS COMMISSION INVESTIGATION

In April of 1980 the Canadian Human Rights Commission sent Patricia Davey to investigate. I had a better feeling right from the start, when I compared this investigator to the investigator from the Public Service Commission's Anti-Discrimination Directorate. The Human Rights Commission came up with their recommendations within a few weeks of investigating, including that there be more female supervisors, and until there were more women supervisors that I be moved elsewhere, and that a fine of fifteen hundred dollars be paid to me for pain and suffering. I was given Davey's recommendations by letter and, by July, a conciliator was appointed.

These recommendations were the first positive news I had received since submitting my complaint. It felt like a minor victory on a long path with very little encouragement! The employer had no obligation to respond. Initially, a conciliator was approved by the union to negotiate a solution with management and a meeting date in late August was set. Three days before it was to be held, National Defence cancelled.

Something I was beginning to notice, though, was that Brennan no longer walked on the base like he owned it, as he had before I made my complaint. I now hardly ever saw him, and when I did see him, he was never alone. He had bought a 1956 red and white Chevy, and once when I happened to be in the office at the same time as he was, he asked me if I liked it. Without thinking I said I did, and I would now always know where he was. There were only two of them in North Bay. Not long after, I heard that he bought another car, one that I did not recognize.

The work environment was very tense, with Brennan taking every opportunity to intimidate me. Sometime after the Human Rights recommendations came through, Brennan came to the cleaner's room in the recreation centre where I worked. The room was about seven feet by twelve feet with no windows. Brennan and the area foreman came in behind me, closed the door, and turned off the light. The room was in total darkness. They said nothing and I just waited. After several minutes, the light was turned on and they left. When later he and the same area foreman asked me to go back to the room, I refused and said whatever he has to say to me he would have to say outside the cleaner's room. They left.

* * *

The same conciliator, who had been chosen by the union for the cancelled meeting with management, asked me to write a letter, on November 4, to the Canadian Human Rights Commission providing them with more detailed information as to why they should hear my complaint at a tribunal. I sat down on that same night and hand wrote a thirteen-page letter and mailed it the next day. This was one of the few handwritten letters (most were typed) I sent during this process. Throughout this time, I had stayed involved in the proceedings, never just assuming things would be taken care of without a certain amount of pressure from me. As much as possible, I also kept notes of what was happening and wrote a great number of letters to the union, the Public Service Commission, women's groups, and the media. I hand wrote my notes with a carbon copy and sent them to Marie McNeely. Most of the letters I sent were typed with several carbon copies in the hopes that the copies would ensure my safety. Challenging the military felt risky. I did not know what they were capable of. If anything happened to me there would be evidence of my complaint. I had started to spread my story around, feeling like there was some safety in numbers. I was figuring out how to be political.

The hearing notice that there was to be a tribunal arrived in January 1981. My complaint would be heard by the Canadian Human Rights Commission. Finally, a real step forward, a real victory! I had recently become involved with the North Bay Women's Centre for support and it felt good to share this victory with them.

I KEEP SHOWING UP

Here it was 1981, and I had worked on the base in this type of isolation for close to two years after the initial reporting of sexual harassment. I was still working with Brennan in a position of power over me. By the time we got to the tribunal, I had already lost sixty days of work due to stress. I had used sick leave and vacation days to cover them. I think my secret weapon and one of my greatest strengths in this struggle, and perhaps one of the most frustrating for management, was the fact that I was still there. I kept showing up to work. One time they were so sure I had quit that the next morning when I came back the area foreman was throwing my things in the dumpster. The things they liked—my scissors, coffee mug, and instant coffee—they had kept. I did make a complaint to the military police but, as I didn't follow up, nothing came of the complaint. I couldn't fight everything.

Every time I got a notice about the hearing, Brennan got a notice, as did the military authorities. I could set my watch after the arrival of these notices by the escalation of the difficulties I would be subjected to.

The preliminary hearing for the Canadian Human Rights Tribunal was on March 17, and I drove to Ottawa to attend. I met my lawyer, K. Scott McLean, for the first time at his office. When we met, he was wearing his yellow motorcycle suit and I immediately felt at ease. Who could be intimidated by someone in a yellow motorcycle suit! He explained what the process was and what would happen. He said that it was not like you see on television. He was going to build my case brick by brick. I had come to the meeting prepared with a copy of the Canadian Human Rights Act, which I was able to give to him, as he did not have a copy at this time. That felt good.

When I returned home on March 18, I found my husband Larry pale and worried. I couldn't imagine what was wrong—I was away for only a couple of days, the kids were not so much work now they were older, and meals were planned. What could be the problem?

It didn't take long to find out. Someone had been to the house attempting to serve me with an action for slander from Brennan. I phoned my lawyer right away. He said it was good news for us and to allow them to serve me when they returned the next day. My lawyer seemed happy with this. I was not. My and Larry's stress levels went up more than a few points.

BRENNAN SUES ME

I waited several weeks before I obtained the Statement of Claim for Brennan's suit. He wanted thirty thousand dollars for damage to his reputation. This was an enormous amount of money for me. And here he was again, claiming that I had done something wrong, while he apparently was going unpunished. I didn't want him to get a dime of our family income for the suffering he had already put me through. I'd also like to note that the amount he was claiming was six times higher than the highest amount allowed at the time for damages by the Human Rights Act. By the time his statement arrived, I had time to get used to Brennan suing me. As the saying goes, I had all my ducks in a row. I had a lawyer; the Human Rights Commission had accepted my complaint; we were going to the Tribunal hearing. Not only was my lawyer not worried, he seemed happy by the suit. I decided not to worry.

When I met McLean in Ottawa before discovery, I signed a document giving him the authority to represent me. That proved to be very fortunate for me as it meant I was able to retain him and the firm he worked for to represent me up to the Supreme Court of Canada.

The search for discovery relating to Brennan suing me was held June 15. Discovery can be granted for one or both sides in a lawsuit and is a pre-trial opportunity for the parties to ask questions and get a sense of the evidence that is going to be used to support their claims or defence. In this case it was my lawyer asking the questions of Brennan to find out how he was going to prove his case against me.

The questioning of Brennan took place on one of the hottest days of the year, and there was no air conditioning in the small room in the roof of the old courthouse in North Bay. I wasn't present during the session, but when McLean came out of that room he told me that he had asked Brennan whether he wore boxers or briefs. He said that line of questioning seemed very disturbing to Brennan, who said "briefs," and that was where my lawyer finished the discovery.

Brennan's lawyer didn't ask to question me. All I know is that McLean said I should have no trouble testifying.

McLean was in town working on both my defence against Brennan's slander suit and for the Canadian Human Rights Commission Tribunal. Because of this, my bill for his time working on the slander suit defence didn't include his travel or any additional hours. I put in a request to the Commission to pay the full bill from McLean on the grounds that if not for my Human Rights complaint going forward, Mr. Brennan would not be suing me. They compromised and paid half the bill. I was responsible for the other half and paid it.

*   *   *

By now, the process had taken on a life of its own. There was no straightforward path to solving my complaint. The goal at this point had become to identify and document circumstances and evidence. I had to have faith this would eventually lead me to a resolution. My union grievance process was dragging on, meeting with resistance at every turn. The Public Service Commission had investigated. The Canadian Human Rights Commission was now involved. Brennan was suing me for slander. Meanwhile, I was working my regular job on the base *and* running around fulfilling requests for this and that from all involved. I just had to get through it all. The idea that this was an orderly "complaints process" would have been laughable, if it wasn't so traumatic. I felt like a piece of meat.

Brennan's authority was only taken away for a short time after my first grievance hearing and never taken away again to my knowledge. Yet, where had it all begun? All I had wanted was to be left alone to do my job. All Brennan had to do was stop. What was the big deal? The process felt like it was moving further away from recognition of the simple fact that Brennan did not stop. I was now two years down the road and no closer to getting any justice. I was learning to live in isolation.

Mid-June things got so bad that I was off work for three weeks. I had already been feeling the pressures were too great for me and earlier, on February 10, 1981, I had been put on anti-depressants by my doctor, which I took until late August. I had been seeing a psychiatrist before the Tribunal started, and during my sessions with him, I had talked about the harassment. With the Tribunal starting, he told me in no uncertain terms that he did not want to be involved in the court's proceedings. I believed that if he were subpoenaed, his testimony about my state of mind would not help me. I had to ask my lawyer not to subpoena him because I did not want to be labelled crazy by my psychiatrist. In the end, he was not subpoenaed and did not testify.

* * *

While I was on holiday in the summer, McLean, acting as the lawyer for the Human Rights Commission, asked me to undergo a lie detector test. As McLean explained to me, I did not have a lot of corroborating evidence and that whatever I could add would be of benefit. Needless to say, I had already realized how unfair the system was and that the entire burden would be on me. The lie detector test was a good idea. To my knowledge Brennan did not take the test himself.

So I left my family and returned to Ottawa to undergo the test at McLean's office. I drove at my own expense and was required to take a hotel room alone. It was not necessarily an unpleasant experience, but I had no choice. I couldn't have known when I began this process what it would cost me in so many ways. This was just another of the many hoops I was required to go through to obtain a remedy. I was desperately trying to prove I was not making it up, because I couldn't prove him guilty. I was told that if I failed the test they would not use it. I did not fail the test.

The complaint process is like a road with many paths leading off from the primary direction. I had to stay on the main path and avoid the branches diverting my energies. Attempting such things as asking the Human Rights Commission to pay for my expenses for the lie detector test was a diversion that could hinder my progress on the main path. I was too stressed and my credibility and energy were too diffused to deal with that kind of detail. So I paid that too.

HUMAN RIGHTS TRIBUNAL HEARINGS BEGIN

In July 1981, the Canadian Human Rights Tribunal hearings began, held in North Bay, before law professor Richard D. Abbott. This first round went for five days, followed in November by three and a half days, and in January 1982, two days were scheduled, but in the end the balance was done by correspondence.

Two years earlier, June 22, 1979, I had put my complaint to management. I could not have imagined at that time I would still be fighting for a resolution, now at the level of a Human Rights Tribunal. The hearings were secret, held *in camera*, at the request of National Defence. This meant they were closed, with no one allowed to be there to support me. To give me courage, I wore a piece of jewellery my father had given to me after my mother's death. By wearing my mother's jewellery, I felt as if she were there with me. It was symbolic but it was the only thing I could do.

The hearing was set up in a courtroom-type setting. I and the other witnesses had to swear under oath to tell the truth. Because it was *in camera* there were no spectators, no press. Other than that, it was what I had expected from watching television, except that my lawyer did not object to repeated questions.

Each time I testified, going over the events, I relived them. Each time, I was again humiliated, belittled, and embarrassed. By the end of my testimony, I was exhausted. When I was told that I couldn't spend time during my lunch break with my long-time friend who was waiting for me, my discouragement turned to despondence. I was so upset after that morning's testimony that I was going to walk in the lake and drown. I have a strong survival instinct, so I'm sure that I would have come to my senses by the time the cold water hit me, but that was what was in my mind. My lawyer drove by me as I was walking and could see by my manner that he should invite me to have lunch with him and his associate. I was not allowed to talk about what went on in court but at least it was company.

In the afternoon of the first day, while being examined by the lawyer for National Defence, I was asked a particular question that kept being repeated, this time for the third time: How many children did I have? I'm not sure how this was relevant at all, and certainly not by the third time. I was angry and feeling pressured by the personal questions, and I answered, "If the number of children I have changes between now and the time I leave this court room I will let you know." That question was not asked again.

My lawyer praised me for this answer and my display of emotion. He was concerned that the anti-depressants I was on were causing me to appear without sympathy and emotionless. Other than this, I don't remember a lot of details of what was said at this first hearing day. I was holding it together reasonably well, but this outburst of mine showed that I was upset by the questioning.

After my testimony, there were others who testified. Some in support of Brennan. The women who testified on behalf of Brennan said they had never been harassed by him, and he had always been a gentleman. In other words, I had to be making it up if he didn't harass every woman there, a point my lawyer later made, stating that just because Brennan hadn't harassed every woman on the base was not proof that he had not sexually harassed me.

None of this testimony surprised me. I'd already encountered it many times. But I had thought I was alone in being targeted. It turned out there were others. It was difficult listening to their testimony. The testimony of one of the female cleaners who had been harassed by Brennan was particularly hard to sit through. I wanted to cry. I could tell she was scared. She was so scared she would not testify with Brennan in the room. To get her to speak, my lawyer told her that Brennan was not there. But he was, just hidden from her view. I found this dishonest. But I guess he had to do what he had to do to get her to testify.

She was afraid because Brennan had apparently hired her on the promise that she would provide sexual favours to him, but she reneged on the promise. By testifying, she was afraid the result would be the loss of her job or reduced or changed hours or other punitive behaviour from Brennan or on his behalf. In fact, after she appeared as a witness she was put on weekends by Brennan, which made it very difficult for her to get to work, as buses did not run early enough for the start of her shift.

At another point in the hearing, my lawyer made the point that even if I had been a terrible cleaner (which I had over and over again proven that I was not), it did not give Brennan an excuse to harass me.

While one of the area foremen was on the stand, he had papers in his hand which he kept referring to during his testimony. Professor Abbott asked him what he was reading and asked to see it. The area foreman was reading from the slander action—he was reading directly off the statement of claim that Brennan's lawyers had filed against me! I and many others in the room were shocked. Professor Abbott asked that this incident and the responses he read from the slander action be stricken from the record. I later checked the transcripts and they had been taken out. It was as though it had never happened, but we all heard him.

On Friday, it was Brennan's turn to testify, but he was not there. He had not returned to the hearing Friday morning, effectively stopping testimony. Thankfully, I had already testified and held my own. No one knew where Brennan was, and it was feared he had taken his life, or at least that is what I was led to believe. As Brennan did not show up, that morning was spent discussing preliminary matters. By noon the hearing was adjourned until November, a full four months away.

UNRELENTING

Since the hearing was adjourned early, the area foreman who had read from the slander action, came up to me and ordered me back to work for the rest of the day. I refused to return to work after such a stressful week and went home. I didn't fill out a leave form. This was my act of defiance. Unusually, I was not disciplined for it or had my pay docked.

The hearing, though, took its toll. I am still stunned at the inhumanity of it. During the most difficult time of the hearing, I was not allowed to talk with anyone. I needed support more than at any other time, and yet I was isolated from that support. My testimony was intimate, embarrassing, and difficult. It was unbearable. And it didn't stop there! After these hearings ended, I still was not permitted to talk to anyone about what happened until my testimony was finished at the hearing in November. This felt almost impossible. I deeply needed to talk about it. Larry and I went to a jewellery store in North Bay, and I bought a gold rope chain. I would rub it to remind myself that I had to stay silent. I still wear it today—but not to stay silent.

I had to go back to work on Monday with the hearing incomplete. There was no way I could be off work until it started up again, as I had used up all my leave. Brennan was still my foreman, still my boss. The retaliation on the job continued, and I felt worse with each passing day.

7

Understanding the Big Picture

T HE REGULAR RHYTHMS OF LIFE DON'T STOP WHEN YOU'RE IN the middle of something like this, much as you may wish they would. A week after the July 1981 hearing of the Canadian Human Rights Tribunal, on the Friday before the August long weekend, my father passed away.

My nerves were taking a beating. I learned of his passing in the morning at work. The area foreman made a point of coming to see me with the collective agreement, just to be sure I knew that I could only have three consecutive days off from the time my father died. The foreman wanted to verify that I knew, because it was a long weekend, that I could only take Friday afternoon off. I told him I would take the time off I needed and put in a leave form on my return. As it turned out, I was back to work on the Tuesday and didn't need to take extra leave.

There was, however, one thing that changed, which helped my return to work. At my request I was allowed a witness of my choice and agreeable to management to be in the same room whenever an area foreman came to see me. The area foreman was constantly badgering me, making it difficult to do my work. He would complain about my work not being done on time or correctly. He would say that I wasn't supervising correctly. He complained about my staff's work. I thought he might be less inclined to harass me in front of a witness, and it would slow him down a little. It did. This lasted until sometime in October and, even though a temporary respite, it did help. But it didn't stop the harassment.

Very few people on the base were not affected by what was happening to me and by Brennan's continued presence. Tension was very high all around.

After the notice for resumption of the hearing was sent out in October, I was presented with an evaluation recommending that I be dismissed. Quick action on my part and that of my lawyer prevented management from acting on that recommendation. Management, apparently, didn't appreciate my resistance, and I was called to the major's office and chastised for phoning my lawyer in Ottawa. I had had enough of being called into his office, and said, "I am just a poor little immigrant girl, why do you keep calling me into the office?" The major said that I was anything but a poor immigrant girl and proceeded to chastise me for calling my lawyer. I saw this as another attempt at intimidation, but one that didn't work. I knew I had a right to call whomever I wished after working hours. The consequence of our quick action was that the written recommendation for my dismissal disappeared so fast it has never resurfaced. However, what did show up on my next performance evaluation was that I was "continually seeking supervisory ability from non DND [Department of National Defence] lawyers" and that I would "refuse when requested to come over to the foreman of the Cleaning Service office pertaining to cleaning matters."

I was also experiencing continued resistance, resentment, and harassment by the cleaners under my supervision in various forms of deliberate insubordination. There seemed to be no end to the bad behaviour by co-workers and no penalties were ever paid. The pattern seemed to be this: if someone wasn't doing their job, I would follow the complaint process as I worked with them to ensure the task was done properly. I would find myself frustrated and would sometimes raise my voice. But eventually, just as we would be getting to a resolution, management would either move me or the individual in question, so there was never any accountability. It undermined my authority and confidence, and I realized there was no way to succeed as a supervisor under these circumstances.

HUMAN RIGHTS TRIBUNAL HEARINGS RESUME

In November 1981, for three and a half days in North Bay, the Canadian Human Rights Tribunal hearings resumed. This time Brennan did testify. He denied ever making any sexual advances to me. I was also put back on the witness stand (not feeling my best, as I was up till 3:30 a.m. the night before writing up my expenses, a last-minute request of my lawyer). The cleaner who testified while Brennan was unnoticed in the hearing room also went on the witness stand to describe the retaliation she suffered after testifying in July. Brennan had changed her shift to weekends at 6:00 a.m., meaning she needed to get a ride from someone else or take a taxi to work. Another cleaner went on the witness stand, stating that a co-worker had been given time off by Brennan as a perk for having testified in his favour. Once all the witnesses had testified, there was only the summations left to be done. Originally, they had been scheduled to take place in Ottawa, three days before Christmas. Much to my relief, due to the illness of one of the lawyers, they were rescheduled for January. I had not been looking forward to travelling out of town so close to Christmas.

As it turned out, the time set aside in January 1982 was still not enough to complete the summation arguments. The balance was done by correspondence, written up and sent to the tribunal chair. The hearings had taken twelve days over a period of five months, and there were still more words to be said.

On February 1, believing my local was unsupportive of my complaint, I asked for representation and assistance from the regional rep in North Bay of the Public Service Alliance of Canada. By February 8, I was sent a letter from the president of the Union of National Defence Employees, local 635, suspending me from my local. True, I was not feeling supported by them, but I was still active and my membership was important to me. My stress level just notched up a bit higher. What was my employer to think if even my local would not support me? I got in touch with Marie McNeely in Kingston and wrote letters to find out on what grounds I had been suspended and demanded a hearing. It took several months to find out the local executive had not liked something I had said at a meeting in November of the previous year, referring to some of the activities of the local executive at a union meeting.

Not willing to fight another battle, I apologized. The first letter of apology was not good enough for them, and I had to write another one before I was reinstated, which was not until December. I had better things to do than to fight with the local.

DECISION: BELIEVED AND NOT HEARD

Finally, on June 30, 1982, law professor Richard Abbott handed down his decision for the Canadian Human Rights Commission Tribunal. In his written statement he concluded, "Her testimony . . . was of such an intimate and embarrassing nature, accompanied by a feeling of humiliation . . . that it could reasonably be expected to be only the truth. Her propensity to tell the truth was confirmed by other evidence." Abbott's take on Brennan, however, was that "he had a severe credibility problem."

This sounds like a win. And it was, according to the Canadian Human Rights Commission. Abbott's decision included a ruling that sexual harassment was discrimination on the basis of sex under the Canadian Human Rights Act. This was the answer the Canadian Human Rights Commission had been waiting for. They wanted confirmation that sexual harassment was considered discrimination, and they got it.

But Abbott's ruling went on to state, "masturbation and fellatio . . . are clearly consistent only with a high degree of voluntary participation . . . I can only surmise . . . that it was not unwelcome." Abbott's opinion was that as repeated sexual acts took place I must have participated voluntarily, therefore there was no sexual harassment. As far as employer liability, Brennan's actions were not actions for which CFB North Bay management (the employer) could be held liable. Abbott therefore dismissed the complaint. The Canadian Human Rights Commission did not appeal the decision, claiming there was not enough evidence. I still don't understand what else they expected to find in the way of evidence.

The decision felt like I had been raped with forty people watching, all saying I must have consented. I never consented and at no time did I say I did. I was believed, but I was not heard.

"MORE THAN MOST WOMEN GET"

The decision left me no dignity and that was all I had left. The hearings were held *in camera*. The only way I could reverse the decision was to appeal to the Canadian Human Rights Review Tribunal. And the only way to keep the testimony and evidence from being destroyed or locked away where no one would see it, as far as I knew, was to appeal the decision on my own.

My lawyer did what he could to talk me out of appealing. He said, "You got your day in court, and that is more than most women get."

This complaint was not about a day in court, it was about restoring my dignity and being treated fairly at work. I appealed the decision to the Canadian Human Rights Review Tribunal before the thirty-day appeal period was up. On July 23, the *North Bay Nugget* reported the Tribunal's decision and my decision to appeal:

> Mr. McLean said today they will appeal to the three-member tribunal. In a 42-page decision released July 5, Mr. Abbott dismissed the case despite "Considerable doubt" in some areas.
>
> Mr. Abbott rejected Mr. Brennan's claim that he did not make sexual advances toward Mrs. Robichaud and that no sexual contact occurred in March, April and May, 1979.
>
> But Mr. Abbott also said Mrs. Robichaud repeatedly told the man his advances were unwelcome, yet each rejection was followed by "sexual encounters in which it must be assumed she participated voluntarily."
>
> He said there was no evidence that Mrs. Robichaud had submitted to the sexual contacts because of threats or promises about her job.
>
> In an interview with *The Nugget* today, Mrs. Robichaud said the decision "really doesn't reflect the evidence in the testimony."
>
> There were 1,600 pages of testimony compiled over 12 days during the hearing.

* * *

Finally, around the same time as the Tribunal decision came down, the grievances I had waited three years for went to the third level and were answered by National Defence. I wasn't surprised about the timing. I assumed it had taken this long because National Defence was waiting to hear the results of the Tribunal. I lost all the grievances, a double blow.

* * *

Larry was remarkable. Work was full of stress and pressure, but my husband was behind me. Larry was a constant source of support. He listened to me and edited my letters. We talked about how to proceed, and he had no complaints about the amount of time and money it was costing us to move forward. The children just coped as best they could while I had a do not disturb sign on my back, and I and their dad dealt with what was happening. At one point my daughter told me that one of the parents of the girls she visited had said that I must have enjoyed being sexually harassed. It was a difficult time for all of us.

Time robbed from our children and the money Larry and I spent on this case was not insignificant. Communications is just one example. It's hard to imagine what it was like before personal computers, the internet, and smart phones. Everything was either mailed or discussed on the phone. Mailed communications involved me writing it out longhand. Then Larry would check it for spelling and grammar, and then I would type it with the appropriate carbon copies. I always kept at least one copy and often made more than one to send to others for information and for safe keeping. Making copies meant using carbon paper. You needed to type with an even pressure to get a clear copy, and if you wanted more than one copy, you had to apply more pressure to your typewriter keys to go through all the layers. And there was no neat way of correcting errors. Then, of course, you had to mail it, which meant paying for postage.

Talking on the phone wasn't cheap, either. It always involved long-distance charges that averaged two hundred dollars a month for six years. When we moved to Ottawa, there were only long-distance calls to people who supported me outside Ottawa. There were no deals on long-distance calls. Every call was timed, and you paid full cost during the day. To get a lower cost, I would have had to call after 6:00 p.m., but that was not an option. Everyone I was talking to was working office hours. With all of the various hearings and appeals, I was spending a lot of time on the phone, either making calls or waiting for calls to come in. We had a big family and finally it got to a point where we put in a second line for the kids. This way I would always have an available line, and they could still call their friends.

* * *

I again wrote the national component office of the Union of National Defence Employees to ask if they would support me. I told them that this time it was just me and the employer. The answer was no. They said it was member (me) against member (Brennan). The national executive voted not to support me, waiting to call the vote until Aileen Manion, the only woman on the executive, had gone to the washroom. Aileen was a strong supporter of women's issues. She passed away not long after that meeting.

Remember where this all began? I had asked for help, and I was the one disciplined. The harasser, to the best of my knowledge, had not been disciplined nor had he asked for help from the union local, but he was offered it.

So here I was, now, appealing the Canadian Human Rights Commission Tribunal decision on my own. I was learning a lot, and the first thing I had to do was hire a lawyer. Luckily, the lawyer who presented my case for the original Tribunal, K. Scott McLean, was retained from an outside firm by the Canadian Human Rights Commission and that contract was complete. I had already hired him to represent me in Brennan's slander action and had an opportunity to evaluate for myself the kind of work he did. He was well organized and knew how to build the case. I sent him a retainer of five hundred dollars.

INSUBORDINATION AND DISOBEDIENCE CHARGES

An appeal of a Canadian Human Rights Commission Tribunal decision is called a Review Tribunal, and the pre-hearing for it took place October 1, 1982. At the same time that the Canadian Human Rights Commission's wheels were slowly turning, for me in my daily work life, the pressure was still on, and Brennan was still my boss. Twice, within a week of each other, I was charged, first with insubordination and then with disobedience.

The insubordination charge was an offence equivalent to the "misuse of explosives causing bodily harm or property damage," and if substantiated, it would mean dismissal. I was devastated by the charge. The lesser charge, that of disobedience, was equally troubling. I can't remember, now, exactly what the offences were that apparently warranted such serious charges. I do remember being accused of not getting the work done that the cleaners I was supervising were ordered but were refusing to do. I already had a heavy workload and could not possibly have completed their work on top of mine. But more than that, even if I had done their work, there would have been certain conflict with the other workers. No matter what I did, I would have had problems.

Whatever the details were, both charges were dropped. One was dropped because the area foreman who laid it didn't appear at the hearing. He stayed off work for six days claiming he was sick, but as a co-worker saw him downtown the day his complaint was to be aired, I am not sure how sick he was. As for the other one, it was dropped due to insufficient evidence.

REVIEW TRIBUNAL DECISION: BRENNAN GUILTY

The Review Tribunal was in Ottawa for only two and a half days in November 1982, and then the waiting started again.

This time the waiting was not long, just until February 21, and this time it was well worth the wait.

The Review Tribunal, consisting of three tribunal members—M.L. Dyer, P.L. Mullins, and W. Robson—ruled that Professor Abbott of the original Tribunal had neglected to question me enough to show whether these acts had taken place with my consent. This time I had been heard. The Review Tribunal stated clearly what I had known all along, that Brennan had harassed and abused me; that he was guilty. Here I quote in some length from the Tribunal decision:

> The Tribunal cannot overlook that the facts clearly showed a pat-
> tern of sexual inquiry and inuendo on the part of Mr. Brennan, and
> his awareness of Mrs. Robichaud's vulnerability as a probationer.
> The cumulative effect was to create a poisoned work environment
> for Mrs. Robichaud. In addition, the facts showed that this pattern
> of harassment and abuse of authority extended not only to Mrs.
> Robichaud but to at least one other female on the cleaning staff.
>
> Accordingly, we have no hesitation in finding that Mr. Brennan
> was guilty of sexual harassment on two grounds:

1) By reason of his failure to rebut the prima facie case established by Mrs. Robichaud;

2) By reason of his creation of a poisoned work environment; both contrary to the Canadian Human Rights Act, Section 7(b).

The Review Tribunal was also clear about the direction they were going in with regard to employer liability. They noted that "Mr. Brennan was the senior civilian managerial employee on the base. The authorities provided to this Tribunal make it quite clear that the liability of the employer for its supervisory personnel is a strict liability."

The February 21, 1983, decision of the Review Tribunal was a landmark decision as it was the first time that a government of Canada department had been found liable for the acts of one of its employees.

A victory and some hard-won relief.

It did not last long.

On Monday, my first day back to work after the decision, I was cleaning the gym floor, driving the Zamboni scrubbing machine. Off and on during the day, there would be a group of military members throwing basket balls into the hoops. This time, they decided I was the target and started throwing them at me. They did stop when I told them they were not permitted to be on the gym floor while I was cleaning, and they left. I guess the news had spread fast and far.

Ten days later National Defence appealed the decision to the Federal Court of Appeal.

BRENNAN STILL MY BOSS

There had been some publicity about the decision in my favour, and I was starting to feel support from a number of areas, including many large unions. I thought this might be the time National Defence would recognize my complaint of sexual harassment at the workplace and, at the very least, fire Brennan. But that just did not happen. National Defence, represented by the Treasury Board, appealed the Review Tribunal's decision. Brennan did not.

Meanwhile, by late February, the RCMP finally started to investigate my complaint of retaliation under what was then section 45 of the Canadian Human Rights Commission (in today's Act, see section 59 "Intimidation or Discrimination"), and in March an investigator arrived. I had all my material ready and, as I remember, he took eleven points from it. Larry and I both attended the interview, which took over two hours. It was good to be allowed the support of Larry, but we had no washroom break, and the process made me feel like I was the criminal.

My complaint was denied. But even if it had been successful, I found out that the RCMP had only six months from the occurrence of the offence to lay charges. Not only were the time limits too short but they were also well past.

8

Pushing beyond Boundaries

EMPLOYERS LIABLE FOR WORKPLACE SEXUAL HARASSMENT

WE WERE NOW ON TO THE NEXT PHASE IN THE PROCESS. THE Federal Court of Appeal had received the Department of National Defence's appeal of the ground-breaking Review Tribunal's decision that the employer could be held liable for sexual harassment by an employee. The Federal Court of Appeal is where Review Tribunals' decisions go if appealed. The appeal would not be scheduled for a hearing until May 1984, over a year away. Dennis Brennan had not appealed the decision that found him guilty of sexual harassment.

My case was gaining attention and support, a lot of it coming from unions and affiliated groups. But so far that hadn't influenced my local or the national executive of the Union of National Defence Employees. They were still not supportive. I was giving up on them and had decided to go ahead on my own. I just didn't have the energy to fight the union and National Defence. I had to do what I call "narrow the enemy" and focus my efforts on the employer.

Luckily though, there was new energy from some of the people I had started to contact. Throughout 1983, I had been in touch with the Women's Committee of Public Service Alliance of Canada, Ottawa–Hull Area Council, and they were giving me much needed support by lobbying the Public Service Alliance to pay my legal fees. And it paid off.

My workload was greatly increased in January. I had the idea to keep daily notes on what I did every two hours. Even though the North Bay regional rep for the Public Service Alliance of Canada advised against it, I kept track of my workload for nine months. Under normal circumstances, I would have met with my supervisors to report what was happening, but they refused to meet with me or talk to me. So I had to write many memos. All of this only helped a little, but it did prevent management from charging me with not doing enough at work. No matter how much I was harassed at work, the workload was still getting done, and my note-taking proved that.

FULL UNION SUPPORT!

On the thirtieth of August, after much pressure from many groups and myself, I got good news. I received a letter from Pierre Samson, national president of the Public Service Alliance of Canada, informing me that they were taking on the responsibility of my legal fees and would reimburse me the forty-eight hundred dollars I had already paid for the Review Tribunal and for expenses involved with the beginning of the Federal Court of Appeal process.

This was good news. I was being fully supported by the Public Service Alliance of Canada. By now I was getting some perspective on how important my case had become. It was no longer only about me, my rights, and my dignity, which were still important to me. My case was now also about stopping sexual harassment at the workplace.

We cannot make social change if nobody knows what it is that needs changing. When I started out on this, I didn't know there was a bigger issue—remember, they told me that this had never happened to anyone else. I was the first one! The union had an important role, and it had to play its part by informing members that this complaint was going through the courts and educating them about its significance.

I finally received real proof and reassurance of the Public Service Alliance's support. On October 19, I received a letter from them informing me that a one-hundred-dollar advance for my travel expenses to Ottawa would be paid and to put in an expense claim while in Ottawa.

I had been invited to speak at the Public Service Alliance of Canada Women's Committee meeting in Ottawa to explain my case. This was the beginning of my public speaking, which was entirely new to me. I guess it went well—there was a good attendance, and I got confirmation that it had been well received. I was invited to the Ontario Federation of Labour, who were holding a confer- ence the following week, and was asked to speak at their "Making Up the Difference" campaign in Ottawa. The campaign was focused on awareness building around the problem of discrimination against women in the workforce. I made it a practice from the beginning to write out my speeches and give a copy to the organizations that invited me. I still have a binder at home with copies of some of the many speeches I made.

The Public Service Alliance of Canada did come through, and on November 7, 1983, I and my family experienced some genuine relief. Their cheque arrived. This was a lot of money—money that we had paid for legal fees for the Review Tribunal and expenses for travel to Ottawa in July. Larry and I were finally able to pay off some of our debt plus have peace of mind knowing the union would from now on be carrying the cost of the legal fees. The costs of long-distance phone calls, postage, photocopying, and some travel were still my responsibility.

Momentum was growing, in terms of union support. I had longed for and desperately needed the support of the union to help me win, and this financial relief was some concrete evidence that they were backing me. "They," however, didn't include my local. The North Bay local was doing far from enough, and I still did not trust them. Being suspended from the union in February 1982 had not helped.

BRENNAN STILL MY BOSS

Despite the building momentum and finally getting some financial relief, the constant harassment at work was unending. My nerves were shot. Unbelievably, Brennan was still my foreman. When my nerves bothered me, I would sing Dutch nursery rhymes while cleaning the washrooms. On one of these very bad days, I went to personnel at CFB North Bay and asked for a resignation form. They couldn't find one; perhaps there wasn't such a form, but perhaps also at this point they didn't want me to quit. When I just wasn't coping, I would take time off on sick leave, but because I carpooled, I would think twice before leaving in the middle of a shift, to either walk home the five miles or drive my car and leave my carpooling partner without a way home. When I was at home, I would cry and cry, then calm down, take on a project, paint a room, clean the basement, or do housework. One time my stress got so bad that I phoned my doctor on a Friday and told him I needed to go to the psychiatric hospital. Thank goodness by Monday, when I was due to go, I had changed my mind and didn't go.

At work, one of the cleaners, my union local president's son, put in a harassment grievance against me. He claimed that I didn't give him permission to go to the bank to cash his paycheque. I had told him he had to finish the work he was doing and then he could go. The situation worried me even though he did not have a leg to stand on. I wanted it handled internally at the local level to save us all a lot of embarrassment, but I failed. It went to a hearing during the week I was making my conference presentations. He lost the grievance. It felt like the only time management showed me any support.

MAKING CONNECTIONS

I had a supervisors' course in St. Hubert, near Montreal, in December, and then took holidays between Christmas and New Year. This was a break of a few weeks and it helped take the pressure off. Even more importantly, it was during this time that I first met Yvonne Seguin.

Yvonne was part of a Montreal organization Groupe d'aide et d'information sur le harcèlement sexuel au travail or GAIHST (Help and Information Centre on Sexual Harassment in the Workplace). I had first heard of this resource group at the Ontario Federation of Labour's "Making Up the Difference" conference in Ottawa. Here I had met someone from Au bas de l'échelle, a grassroots organization in Quebec working for the rights of non-unionized workers, who had told me about GAIHST. This centre was created in 1980 by a group of women who had been subjected to sexual harassment at work and had tried to seek help, only to find help did not exist. They were told it was a personal problem and to deal with it on their own, something I could relate to. So these women decided to create a committee and eventually a not-for-profit organization whose objective was to sensitize the population on sexual harassment at work and to provide support to women experiencing sexual harassment at work. I was so glad they were there, and Yvonne was a key support throughout the rest of the years. To this day, she's still my best friend.

Yvonne hosted me over the weekend break—the course ran over two weeks, and we had the middle weekend off. Someone at the supervisors' course gave me a ride to Yvonne's home and picked me back up on Monday morning. This was the first time I had a chance to talk in depth with someone who understood sexual harassment. I was hugely relieved, very emotional, and I learned a lot.

My other activities were also gathering momentum. When I went to the 1983 Ontario Federation of Labour conference in Ottawa, I had provided the organizers with an outline of what was happening at my workplace. In May 1984, their women's news bulletin's "Making Up the Difference" campaign report published the brief I had presented in Ottawa. Before I even knew it had been published, they sent a copy to my union steward. He worked in supply, where he received and provided linens for making the beds. His work station had a wide counter between the people picking up and leaving sheets. To this day I am glad for that counter between the two of us. I don't know what would have happened without that obstacle keeping him at a distance. He sure was angry about my report being published.

The Ontario Federation of Labour had also sent letters to MP Herb Gray (president of the Treasury Board) and Jean-Jacques Blais (my MP, who was also Minister of National Defence) requesting that the Treasury Board drop their appeal of the Review Tribunal's decision.

A BREAK FROM BRENNAN

Back at work, in February, I was offered a transfer to Public Works Canada, another department of the federal government. I received a lot of pressure from the Public Service Alliance regional rep to take it, with encouragement like, "If you don't take it, you will be up shit creek without a paddle," which made me suspicious, and I turned it down. Good thing too—less than a year later that position and others were declared surplus, and I would have been unemployed.

Shortly after, I was offered a secondment to the Martin Leo Troy Armoury in North Bay. This seemed a better option. A secondment meant that I was still guaranteed my job on the base once the court's decisions were resolved, and in the meantime, I could get a bit of relief from the unending pressure at CFB North Bay. I decided to take it. Brennan, meanwhile, continued to work his regular job, just without me to hassle.

I started February 15, 1984, and was immediately very relieved. It was the psychological rest I needed. It's not like I was welcomed or needed at the armoury—I wasn't. I wasn't even given a key to my cleaner's room. I ate lunch alone and was told that I could watch television, knit, or walk the grounds. I even got the idea to sign up at the high school next door to take a Shakespeare class. This didn't last long, before I was told that I couldn't take a full hour's break all at one time.

When I did get a chance to talk with the supervisor there, I learned that he felt slighted because the difference in our pay was so little. I suggested that he see his union representative and put in a classification grievance, which he did and got a raise and back pay.

*   *   *

In December 1983, Larry and I had written to *W5*, a popular national television current affairs program, about my complaint of sexual harassment and asked if they would like to do a story. We heard from them in February of the following year. Yes! They would take it on and would be sending someone to North Bay to set up the show. We barely had time to register what this meant before they were there with their crew. The filming went from February 29 to March 2—very exciting and affirming and the airing of the story was a dream come true. For the filming, I was interviewed in my living room, on the work site, and they even had me drive my truck to the North Bay Mall, across from where Brennan lived. Some of my co-workers were also interviewed, and the *W5* crew waited outside Brennan's apartment building to get his comments. All he said was "I have nothing to say right now." The show aired March 11, 1984, which felt great. My life was full of contrasts, though. I went from the highs of national recognition for the effort I was putting in to stop workplace sexual harassment, back to the daily reality of harassment and isolation at work and resistance from my union local.

The Public Service Alliance of Canada and Union of National Defence Employees' national executive and staff travelled to North Bay February 13 to meet with me and the local executive to ensure I had representation from them regarding my sexual harassment complaint. It was a mistake for me to meet with them without my own support. The meeting was held at the Public Service Alliance's regional office in North Bay. There were six of them—and me. They represented the union top brass. From the Public Service Alliance of Canada: 4th vice-president, grievance and adjudication officer, and regional rep; and from the Union of National Defence Employees: national president, local 635 president, and a female steward, who was hoping to represent me.

It was a long and difficult meeting, which did not end until 7:45 p.m. There was a lot of time spent arguing about my going to the Ontario Federation of Labour for support and publicity and also about my status as a union steward. I had understood that when I was reinstated in the local I was again a steward, but the local president wanted to be sure I understood that was not the case. They argued that I was not made of the "right stuff" to be a steward. Representation by the union local for my sexual harassment complaint was another issue that took a lot of time. They tried to get me to accept representation from the local, but the woman who could represent me would not see me without a witness. I didn't trust someone who didn't trust me enough to be in my company without a witness. And I was not confident that she had the knowledge required to represent me, and I wasn't going to gamble my job on her ability to do so. In the end, I refused to accept the representation that was offered. After the meeting they all went out to an expensive dinner together, and I went home alone.

I felt very isolated and realized that I should never have gone to that kind of meeting alone. The meeting turned out a dismal failure. I was so traumatized afterward that I had nightmares and found it difficult to go to work the next day. It was my last day of work on the base before my transfer to the armoury.

I was scheduled to be at Canadian Labour Congress trade union school for the week of March 18 to 23, 1984, but only two days before I was due to leave I was blocked from going by the regional rep under pressure from the local. I did succeed in going to a Canadian Employment and Immigration Union Women's Conference in Toronto and gained a lot of support there.

As my problem with the local was far from resolved, another meeting was set for Ottawa, March 28. Although the process was not much better than the first meeting, it did have a positive outcome, with Public Service Alliance of Canada agreeing to report on the upcoming Federal Court of Appeal hearing and to publish information about it. They would also encourage members to attend. These were important steps forward. Up to this point, it was as if there was a zone of silence in this union and around North Bay, as my local had so strongly resisted informing members about my case and the issues involved. But my problems with the local weren't over.

In late April, I went to the Ontario Federation of Labour Women's Lobby and Conference in Toronto, where my story was presented in their brief, a proud moment for me. I didn't stay for the end of the conference, though, as I was having such a difficult time dealing with my local's non-support. For example, normally, the expenses for these conferences would be paid for by the local, but I had to pay it all out of my own pocket. To save me the cost of a hotel and to help me feel supported, I would often take a billet (meaning union members would offer conference attendees a place to stay in their homes).

Before I left, though, I had a good talk with the Ontario Federation of Labour's human rights director, where I cried my eyes out. Afterward, blurry eyed, I drove the two hundred and fifty miles home. I was in rough shape. I don't know how I made it.

*   *   *

A few days after the Ontario Federation of Labour conference in Toronto, on May 1, 1984, the Federal Court of Appeal hearing was held in Ottawa, in the Supreme Court of Canada building. During the reading of the complaint by one of the three judges, I saw them smile and smirk. It was very uncomfortable to think that these men were going to decide the fate of my complaint. I needn't have worried, yet. Almost immediately, the hearing was adjourned and postponed. Brennan, who had thought National Defence was appealing on his behalf, was informed that he had to appeal on his own behalf to the Federal Court of Appeal, and he was to have had the proper papers filed in advance. Now seventeen months after the Review Tribunal decision—long past the allowed "ten calendar days"—his appeal would be allowed to be heard.

There was a wonderful part about this brief moment in court before we were adjourned. Before the hearing, I had asked my lawyer if the hearing room was large. He said yes, but hadn't elaborated. When I got there, I found that what he meant was that the room was at least three stories high from floor to ceiling, and it was filled to capacity! Most in attendance were women, but with some men, all wearing yellow roses. Bobbi Sparks, a National Defence union local president from Kingston, who had organized a bus with support from other union members, was responsible for a lot of this. Some people were also wearing buttons, "PSAC against Sexual Harassment," made by a Public Service Alliance of Canada Sudbury local. The courtroom was so crowded that I sat in the front with my lawyer rather than in the benches with the observers. To show support the people who could not enter due to overcrowding waited outside, and they too were all wearing yellow roses.

This tremendous show of support had to see me through many difficult months of waiting for the hearing to be rescheduled.

One day, I came home from work early and very discouraged. I felt no one loved me, not even me. My dog Sam, my friend from my Tupperware days, insisted that wasn't true—he was waiting for me outside the door, just wagging his tail and being so happy to see me. When I checked the mail there was an envelope with a five-hundred-dollar donation from Canadian Employment and Immigration Union component president. Sam and that cheque got me through another tough day. The donation motivated me to ask the Public Service Alliance of Canada to make buttons against sexual harassment and, within two months, they did.

The Ontario Federation of Labour had set up a "Bonnie Robichaud Defence Committee" to help out with expenses, since my local was failing to properly represent me. It was a great strength to have support from other unions and women's and community groups. In fact, without it I'm not sure how I could have kept going.

There were real gains achieved in the workplace influenced by my case as we waited for the appeal to resume. The Treasury Board issued a policy against personal harassment at the workplace and many unions, including the Public Service Alliance of Canada, worked (successfully, in some places) to incorporate clauses prohibiting discrimination and sexual harassment in their collective agreements. The problem of sexual harassment at a workplace would never be easy to solve, but it was being perceived more and more as a legitimate complaint. Attitudes were slowly changing, and I felt real progress was being made, bringing women some equality on the job.

The Public Service Alliance of Canada requested yet another meeting that was held in North Bay with my local, July 20, 1984. Again, it was unsuccessful. At that point, I decided to only work on gaining support and publicizing my case. It was hard to give up trying to get my local on side, but it was beginning to feel futile. I said to them and a union national officer, "I am going to win this with the employer first, and I will come back and see you later."

MY DEFENCE COMMITTEE NEWSLETTER

The Federal Court of Appeal hearing date was once again announced, this time for September. This meant I had to get through the summer and make good use of it. I had an idea. I needed a photocopier and tried to rent one for a few months. This proved impossible, so I decided to buy one. When I brought it home, I wondered what had taken me so long! It had become too time consuming to send individual letters to all the contacts I had made over the years. I could no longer afford all the long-distance calls, so I started the "Bonnie Robichaud Defence Committee Newsletter." About a year later, I bought a computer and printer, which made it easier for me to correct errors, and I no longer needed to use carbon paper as I now had a photocopier.

The board of directors of the Public Service Alliance of Canada were among the recipients of my first newsletter. It was time they heard about me from me. Although they had agreed at the March meeting to inform members about the Federal Court of Appeal hearing, they were still treating my complaint in a confidential manner and, as a result, they (and the members) did not know what was happening. I also decided to put the newly elected Mulroney cabinet ministers, the news media contacts I had gathered, and unions and women's groups on the mailing list. By the time I was done I had a mailing list of about two hundred people and organizations. I was nervous putting out that first issue in October 1984; I was already being sued. But once it was copied and in the envelopes, I was not changing my mind.

My list of supporters in that first newsletter included the Public Service Alliance's Women's Committee Ottawa–Hull Area Council; Ontario Federation of Labour; Canadian Labour Congress; North Bay Women's Centre; Ontario Public Service Employees' Union; National Action Committee on the Status of Women; Union of National Defence Employees locals from Sudbury, Kingston, and Toronto; and MPs Lynn McDonald, Terry Sergeant, and others.

I asked all those who received my newsletter to write letters of support to politicians, their unions, media representatives, and anyone else they thought may have influence, and even included sample letters.

I was starting to get support from a broad section of the labour movement as a result of the wide distribution of my newsletters. Donations were growing. My media contacts meant many newspaper articles were being published. Reporters follow what is going on in the courts and that helped to get their attention. I was also speaking at events such as union meetings, women's groups, and schools. I had many radio, television, and newspaper interviews. All the while, I did whatever I could to increase my knowledge of sexual harassment, which by this time, I understood was not limited to my experience.

9

Going It Alone

SEPTEMBER 1984 FINALLY ROLLED AROUND, AND WE WERE BACK in Ottawa, at the Federal Court of Appeal. I wasn't finding the hearings any easier to sit through. The Treasury Board case, from what I could gather, seemed to hinge on the idea that I hadn't given my employer the details of the harassment. I knew full well that management had refused to listen when I did give them the details, with Captain Adlard telling me he was coming out of a divorce and didn't want to deal with such things at work.

They also argued that I hadn't made the complaint right after the end of my probation for promotion to lead hand. Truth is, I had started talking about it almost immediately after the end of my probation, starting with my family doctor and my husband, followed not long after by a written statement of being sexually harassed to an official of my union local. It wasn't long after that that I filed my official complaint. Not that any of this is the point, which is that the end of my probation did not make speaking out against Brennan a lot easier. It only meant there was one less barrier. National Defence's argument was just another blame the victim strategy.

The afternoon was spent repeating over and over again all the details of sexual contact. This is always traumatic. I won't repeat them again here—I outline them in detail in chapter 3 of this book because I think it's important for people to know what sexual harassment can look like and feel like. It was a nightmare. During the process of getting to the Supreme Court, I had had to relive it dozens of times. It is never easier.

Brennan's lawyer, Mr. Sangster, finished his arguments at the end of the morning on the second day. Brennan never returned to court after the May 1, 1984, hearing.

My lawyer, K. Scott McLean, started his case in the afternoon. Among other arguments, he pointed to a "Confidential Memorandum" by the base commander that said that I was to be made an example of and to keep a file on me. The memo said that because I had won three of the nine grievances, it would appear that the union had won (see chapter 5). McLean also noted that during the grievance process management had said that they would destroy a number of letters of complaints and two petitions made against me and kept in my file. These had been found to have been organized by Brennan and not to have been made in good faith. The letters and petitions were torn into three pieces each, in front of me and my witness, Marie McNeely. As I've already related, at the time I noted to Marie that I didn't want these destroyed and that tearing them into three pieces was not what I would call destroyed. Well—surprise!—during discovery, McLean found these items had been taped back together and kept in my file all along. In this case their bad faith was backfiring.

McLean finished on Friday and was followed by Russell Juriantz, who presented arguments on law. At 4:30, the hearing was adjourned till November 23. After a full day of hearing on November 23, the hearings were completed.

I gave a full report of the September hearings in my second newsletter and, with the help of my photocopier, distributed it widely.

* * *

In February 1985, the Federal Court of Appeal ruled on whether they would allow National Defence's and Brennan's appeals. They found Dennis Brennan liable and denied his appeal. This also meant, as my lawyer told me later, that finally Brennan's slander suit against me would be stayed. Although this part of the appeal's decision was a victory for me, the fact that National Defence's appeal was allowed meant there would be no celebration. I still had work to do and I still had an unsafe workplace environment.

National Defence's appeal was allowed on a split decision, with two judges of the three ruling in their favour. They said the Department of National Defence could only be liable if the Minister of Defence or the Treasury Board president had sexually harassed me or had ordered someone under their command to do so, which to me was ridiculous. Justice MacGuigan, the dissenting judge, said that only the employer could rectify the wrong; the harasser could not do it.

To my mind, the importance of establishing employer liability cannot be overemphasized. The Canadian Human Rights Act was amended after the Review Tribunal decision of 1983 to include employer liability. Complaints made before that time, including mine, would not benefit from that change, which meant that an employer could merely claim to be unaware, to look the other way when these incidents occurred and simply state that they did not know or authorize it.

I APPEAL TO THE SUPREME COURT

I immediately asked for leave to appeal to the Supreme Court of

Canada. But that was not as easy as it sounds. First, I had to convince my lawyer to take the case, and then I had to go to the bank and get a loan to send him a thousand-dollar retainer to proceed. When I spoke to an elected representative on the national executive of the Public Service Alliance of Canada, he told me I could not appeal. I said "Oh yes, I can decide to appeal and you can decide to pay." I asked the Alliance for support but was concerned that if they took too much time to decide that the ninety-day appeal period might run out. Time had to be allowed to prepare the appeal, and it would be too late. I was not prepared to risk this happening, so I appealed first and hoped the Alliance would follow with my legal fees. One month later I was granted their support, and the Public Service Alliance of Canada reimbursed me the thousand-dollar retainer I had sent my lawyer.

Just before the first ever Public Service Alliance of Canada National Women's Conference, held in Ottawa, my component president of the Union of National Defence Employees informed me by phone that I was not allowed to go. This was his first and only phone call to me. I remembered how I was not allowed to go to the Canadian Labour Congress trade union school the year before, so I said to myself, "Not this time." I told him I was going and had already paid the fee. He said he would refund me the thirty-five dollars I had paid. I said, "No you won't, I am going to be there inside and welcome with other delegates, or outside with a picket sign, but either way I will be there." As it turned out, I didn't need a picket sign. I was inside and welcome.

The conference was difficult for me, but I stayed for the duration. On the last day, I managed to find enough people to have my question of support brought to the table, and the hat was passed with nearly one thousand dollars raised. Again, I had gone without the support of my local for leave without pay, travel, and hotel costs, meals, and a daily minimum. The donations that day from my sisters and their locals were such a welcome relief.

After the conference I had to go straight to Montreal for the taping of the *Brian Gazzard Show*, a current affairs program on television. I jumped in my truck and just drove straight there, not daring to stop on route. All the donations I received were in cash, and I had never carried that much money at any one time in my life! I stayed with Yvonne Seguin, and I sure was excited when I got there.

The next morning, we went to the bank to have the money converted to a cashier's cheque for safekeeping, and that afternoon we went for the taping of the show. All the make-up was put on, but at the last minute it was decided to film in the evening instead. The studio audience was too small, so we went back again that night. The

April 1, 1985. Bonnie attends the PSAC Women's Conference without union support.

taping went well, but the audience was tough. One woman stood up and asked what type of husband I had that would let me work in a place like that! Thankfully there were also some good questions.

BRENNAN STILL (AGAIN) MY BOSS

Around this time, I requested an end to my secondment at the Troy Armoury. I had been glad to have the break from Brennan, but the situation was deteriorating. Early in the summer of 1984, my co-worker cleaner burnt his arm and was off for some time. Not long after he returned, in September, the foreman became ill and didn't return, which left my co-worker as a supervisor over me, a role he wasn't comfortable in. As much as possible, we kept clear of each other, but he became unreliable and unpredictable. It was his job to open up in the morning, and without his keys I couldn't get in. From my observations it became obvious that his use of alcohol was impinging on his work. I didn't have any experience dealing with this and when it threatened my work, I reported him. Nothing came of it, and as the situation got worse, eventually I requested to be transferred back to the base.

The Federal Court of Appeal decision was rendered on February 17, 1985, and Brennan, despite being found liable for sexual harassment, was still the foreman and once again my supervisor. The decision should have meant immediate dismissal as promised in the first-level grievance reply. But this did not happen. I returned to hostile working conditions. Some of my co-workers and the staff that I supervised were openly rude to me. Once when I assigned work to a member of my staff, he refused the work by saying, "I am not your husband or your lover." The area foreman did support me in that situation, saying that he shouldn't have said that, but he took no further action. The damage was done.

* * *

I had been in correspondence with P.D. Fitzmaurice, the director of the Anti-Discrimination Directorate of the Public Service Commission's appeals and investigation branch. He wanted more and more information and documentation from me, which I had been sending. I was completely worn down. After a telephone conversation with him on March 29, 1985, I realized that I didn't have the energy to help him anymore and wrote him the following:

> I started to go through my files. I found it painful beyond endurance. If you wish an investigator to review and or make copies of my files please feel free to do so. . . .
>
> Perhaps at some later time when I feel stronger, I can deal with the material you request, but not at this time. For the present time I am going to see my doctor with the aim of taking time off on sick leave, and applying for Workers' Compensation. I must use all the courage I possess to keep up my morale and stay alive for the children we are raising and hope somehow there will be better times. It does not seem to matter what I say or what I do, nothing seems to do the trick to give me equality in the workplace. My Supervisor does not even know he is harassing me. I certainly think it is high time that education is done at C.F.B. North Bay Re: discrimination and harassment as they don't even know what they are doing.
>
> As for me I know I have done all that I can possibly do and so much more to achieve a harassment-free workplace. For me at least I cannot now envision a day when that might ever happen, and without that hope I cannot go on.
>
> I wish I could do more, but for now I can do no more. I still live in hope that perhaps an investigator can come to North Bay and

recognize and correct the problems I face at work. When I can do more, I will write again.

In April, I went on leave for about four weeks. That was the last of my sick leave. I had to go back to work despite the constant harassment and sexist attitude of Brennan and staff.

It was hard to believe Brennan, despite being found liable for sexual harassment, was allowed to continue being my foreman. I put in yet another complaint to the Public Service Commission, but there was no change. I felt cheated that I was suffering so much at work yet he had no repercussions. It was a very difficult time. I had no relief, and I felt nothing was truly resolved, even though there had been rulings in my favour. I wrote National Defence management to say that at the very least Brennan should not be my boss.

On May 23, 1985, the Supreme Court of Canada granted leave to appeal the issue of employer liability. This was a big relief. Again, I could believe that momentum was building—and with nowhere to go if you lose at Supreme Court, it was now or never.

SUSPENDED WITHOUT PAY

I believe that the momentum I was starting to gain had something to do with the fact that on May 30, a week after being granted my appeal at Supreme Court, I was suspended without pay. It turned out that Brennan was also suspended at around the same time. It was as if National Defence could easily punish *me* without touching Brennan, but the instant they decided to hold Brennan responsible for something, they couldn't do it without "equally" punishing me.

My suspension originated from a discussion with one of my cleaners. He asked me if I had heard about Brennan, and I said no but that I was aware there was a representative of the Public Service Commission on the base doing an investigation. That seemed to make him upset. Before I knew it, he was shouting at me, and I was raising my voice. He said he wanted to see the major, and I said fine. He called and got an appointment right away, and because I had experience with how hard it was for me to get an appointment anytime, I knew I was in trouble.

I went back to my regular work area only to be found by my area foreman who told me the major wanted to see me. I could have refused, as by this time my shift was over, but decided to go. At this meeting I was told Brennan had been suspended, which was a welcome surprise. I was also asked if I was going to be into work the next day. I said I would be in. The next morning the same employee and I again had words, and I gave him a verbal warning as his supervisor.

By midmorning I was called into base headquarters. I was sure that there would be discipline involved. It was a beautiful warm sunny day. To calm myself before going into headquarters I stood and breathed slowly, taking the time to look at the trees. When I arrived at the meeting, I asked if this was a disciplinary meeting. The answer was "yes." So I asked, "Whose discipline?" Mine, I was told. I was asked to sit, but refused. I wanted to show my defiance and to be taller than the man from human resources. This bothered him a lot. I was then handed a letter, which read: "You are hereby suspended without pay pending the outcome of a complete investigation into the disturbances of 29 and 30 May 1985 at your work locations," and it was signed by the base commander. Had they done a complete investigation into my complaint of sexual harassment things might have turned out differently for me.

This suspension was very difficult for me. It seemed to me National Defence on one hand was finally taking my complaint seriously and believing Brennan to be a liability, while on the other hand decided to treat us both as troublemakers and suspend us both. All this time, since I filed my complaint in 1979, National Defence had seemed to be fine with various disciplinary actions against me alone. So now that they were forced to discipline Brennan, why did they also need to come down hard on me? Once again there was no support from management for me to do my job as a lead hand. I believed they wanted both of us off the base.

Ironically, I had been advised by the Public Service Commission's representative to be assertive when a cleaner gave me a hard time, to raise my voice to ensure they would listen to me and follow my instructions. The cleaner had stated in his grievance that I was blocking his exit. As I had my back against the wall, his exit was not blocked. I believed a suspension without pay following an argument was excessive and had some confidence that it would be resolved in my favour. I thought this was a knee-jerk reaction by National Defence following the approval of leave by the Supreme Court that my case was worth hearing.

Several days later I was ordered to undergo a psychiatric assessment at the then government Department of Health and Welfare, in Toronto. I refused and also refused to sign forms giving them my medical information. I did go to see my psychiatrist in North Bay. My family doctor got the report and affirmed I was of sound mind and health.

NEWSLETTER MAKING WAVES

Meanwhile, my newsletters were paying off, with a growing network of recipients in the labour movement and beyond. I was getting donations and letters of support from many sources. Many groups also sent copies of the newsletter out to their own mailing lists. I had produced six newsletters to date, and the mailing list had grown to five hundred. The newsletter was very successful in raising funds for my out-of-pocket expenses, such as mailing, long-distance phone calls, paper, and so on. Over the six months there was a total of about five thousand dollars donated from unions, individuals, and women's groups.

I had developed a rapport with the media. I routinely mailed out press releases and any other material I thought would be useful to them. I made myself available to speak to them when requested, often speaking on radio interviews for the national public broadcaster, CBC, and others. I travelled to Ottawa to be on *Canada AM*, a popular morning television news program, and to Toronto to be on the *National*, CBC's evening television news program.

Many newspapers, such as the *North Bay Nugget*, *Toronto Star*, and *Ottawa Citizen*, among others, were following the story and publishing articles. Some asked me to provide material—my picture and that of the children at the age they were when the complaint was first made.

I was still being asked to speak at various unions, women's groups, and schools—which I continued for a few years after the Supreme Court decision in 1987. All the while I did whatever I could to build support and knowledge of sexual harassment.

The suspension and order to have a psychiatric assessment all happened on the eve of sending out my latest Defence Committee newsletter.

It was to be the last one sent for two years.

At home, I was dealing with the reality of being on leave without pay. On June 7, I had received an actual pink slip. Larry insisted that I apply for what was then called unemployment insurance, or UI. This was not my choice. It was bad enough that I was told that I was on leave without pay, but applying for unemployment insurance felt like an additional humiliation. I went to the employment office downtown, put in my application, and spoke to a councillor who told me that I must prove I was looking for work. I had to give them signed copies of my job applications. Every two weeks I had to send in cards and the results of my employment search. I never received any unemployment payments, though I fulfilled all the requirements to collect. On the good side, I never had to return any, either.

About nine weeks after first applying for UI, I was told I had won my grievance on the suspension without pay. I learned it on a Thursday at 4:00 p.m. I was happy about that. I thought 4:00 p.m. was too late to phone the employment office to tell them I was no longer unemployed, so I called them the next morning. Apparently, that wasn't fast enough. I quickly received a letter from the employment office stating that I was illegally trying to collect UI by not immediately reporting my reinstatement. I'm guessing this is one of those things that can happen in a small town. Maybe someone in the office knew what was going on with my case and wasn't happy about it. Whatever, that letter felt tacky.

The only time that I begrudged spending money on stamps is the money I spent on the stamps I used to send in with my job search.

All through these years, Larry and I were tight for money. The money we were receiving in donations through my outreach helped a lot, but we still had many uncovered out-of-pocket expenses. We were spending a lot of money on fighting the complaint. To help make up for the income lost because of my unpaid suspension, Larry and I decided to sell the travel trailer. This was not an easy decision. It carried many happy memories for me and my family.

SUSPENSION LIFTED

At some point during the process, I did finally get representation from the Public Service Alliance of Canada's regional rep for my suspension without pay and, by early August, my grievances against the suspension were upheld. I was given all the back pay for the suspension period plus three additional paid weeks off. To receive my first cheque owed me, I was escorted onto the base by the regional rep. He was uncomfortable when I spoke to other cleaners, and it was clear that he did not want the other cleaners to know that I had won the grievances. The second time, while I was still off work, when the remaining pay was due to me, I was not allowed to go on base.

The regional rep was also the one who told me that to continue to negotiate my complaint with the Public Service Commission I had to stop publishing and distributing my newsletter. I regret agreeing to this condition. It meant I was cut off from my main support and them from me.

This didn't mean, though, that I stopped communicating, particularly with the press. I continued to send out press releases to major newspapers such as the *Toronto Star* and *Ottawa Citizen*. By the end of the summer several newspapers had published feature length articles.

10
Choosing to Fight, Again

D ESPITE THE PAUSE IN MY NEWSLETTER PRODUCTION, I WAS
still getting a lot of media coverage, both local and national. In
my opinion, as a result of all the media coverage of my case, National
Defence was finding itself under a lot of pressure from public opinion to proceed with negotiations. The first meeting to discuss the
results of my complaints with the Public Service Commission took
place in August (after all the media coverage). After a presentation to
the House of Commons Subcommittee on Equality by the Human
Rights Institute of Canada and more media articles, many drawing
attention to my May 30 suspension without pay, there was another
meeting of National Defence and the Public Service Alliance of
Canada, on August 19, 1985.

TENTATIVE AGREEMENT

During that meeting, a tentative agreement was reached, giving me
three years leave with pay and money for tuition and books to attend
Nipissing University College. At no time during the discussion or in
that tentative agreement was there any mention of giving up my right
to appeal to the Supreme Court of Canada. That is something I would

never have agreed to. I would not even have agreed to come to a meeting if I had thought that's what they wanted.

There were conditions, though. I would only be allowed to take a leave of absence from my job to pursue formal education *if* I also gave up various complaints, such as my new section 45 complaint for being put on leave without pay only days after getting leave to appeal to the Supreme Court and another complaint I had made to the Canadian Human Rights Commission (see chapter 9) for being suspended without pay. There was pressure on me to give up issues that included seeking damages against my boss, Brennan, and the Department of National Defence. It's also my opinion that in these negotiations, there was an element of retaliation by National Defence for my challenge to the Supreme Court and other union-related complaints, shown by, for example, their condition that I could apply for a job in another federal department but not in the Department of National Defence.

Bonnie and Larry, October 1985, at the office of the Canadian Human Rights Institute in Ottawa.

After the suspension had been lifted, and I had used up the additional paid time off granted to me, I finally returned to work on September 4, 1985. Meanwhile, I had not been idle. I had been in touch for some months with Dr. Marguerite E. Ritchie, president of the Human Rights Institute of Canada, and I wrote to her again on October 7 to lobby my case. I ended my letter with this: "I sincerely hope by the time you get this letter National Defence will have run out of deadlines. If not I am sure I will have run out of energy and I need answers for the most positive results possible: a harassment-free workplace without me the victim having to leave, no matter how nicely it is done."

I phoned my lawyer to make an appointment and got one on October 17, a Thursday.

APPEAL OR EDUCATION—THE DEVIL'S BARGAIN?

That letter to Dr. Ritchie was sent only days before I was to sign the first agreement, already at my lawyer's office when I arrived. I was prepared to sign the agreement with its conditions, but only if I was assured that it was to have an addendum signed by National Defence ensuring I could take my complaint to the Supreme Court of Canada.

A week later I was told by my lawyer that National Defence had decided they would *not* sign the addendum. I was devastated and livid.

During this time, I had already enrolled in university and, when my work schedule allowed, was attending classes, taking computer science, business English, an accounting course, philosophy, and geography. Now this. I had to choose—I could go to school, graduate, get a new job, and hope to put everything behind me; or I would stay where I was, isolated and under constant surveillance and threat of discipline, but able to take the issue of employer liability to the Supreme Court of Canada.

I couldn't separate the sexual and general harassment I received from Brennan while my employer looked the other way from this bigger issue of a harassment-free workplace for women. All I could manage at this point was to cry. My lawyer told me to think it over for the weekend and let him know on Monday.

I had not even taken a copy of the agreement home with me because it was secret and I thought if I did not have a copy then I could not tell anyone about it.

On Sunday, I managed to reach Dr. Ritchie who suggested that I drive from North Bay to Ottawa first thing Monday morning, get a copy of the agreement, and then decide what to do next. Monday morning Larry and I got up at 5 a.m. and arrived at Dr. Ritchie's about 9:30 a.m. From there we went to my lawyer's office, where his secretary gave me a copy of the agreement. Back at Dr. Ritchie's office, we talked things over. I was extremely upset. My lawyer asked for a week's extension to give me time to find out more information.

Before I left Ottawa, I went to the national office of the Public Service Alliance of Canada and spoke with staff and executive members. They told me that they would continue to support me, but that the Public Service Commission would drop my complaint if I did not sign. My lawyer had already said he would no longer represent me if I did not sign the agreement. He felt it was the best I could do. Larry and I travelled back home to North Bay that night with heavy hearts. An executive officer from the Public Service Alliance called me Tuesday night to say I should accept the education plan, that I had done enough for my brothers and sisters in the union. I told her I was on my way to class and did not want to be late and I would sleep on it.

It was all I could do to make it through that class. I cried all the way home. That night I cried myself to sleep. I had decided not to sign the agreement, and I knew it was the right decision. The next day I spoke to the Canadian Human Rights Commission lawyer who said I was not likely to succeed in the Supreme Court if I signed away my right to go. When I got that information, I phoned my lawyer and left a message with his secretary that I was turning down the agreement.

I had just read Margaret Atwood's newly published book

The Handmaids Tale, and a thought struck me—women in that book did not have a choice, but I did. I still had the right to appeal.

My decision was made. It was still early in the day, and I began writing my press release announcing that I was going back to work and not accepting the agreement. I called Dr. Ritchie in Ottawa and read it to her. She said it was marvellous.

I then decided to call the negotiator P.D. Fitzmaurice to verify that the Public Service Commission was dropping my complaint. I also had another motive to call him. He had been so attentive and helpful during the previous months, I thought I owed it to him to let him know. I read him my press release, and he was upset that I had written that the agreement had been achieved through trickery and deceit. I said, "Well that's what I think." He then told me I would have to write the others who had signed the agreement before I could put the press release out. I said, "Fine, give me their addresses."

I thought I must have to have my head examined to be turning down such an opportunity! University was good for me. At the same time, my mind was at ease and I was not going to change it. At some point in the afternoon, I got a call from Larry's work and he had had an epileptic seizure. I needed to go and get him.

When we arrived home the phone was ringing off the hook— we didn't have an answering machine, and it was before they or cell phones were common. The first call I got was from a national executive officer of the Public Service Alliance. He said they were making a change to the agreement and read me a clause allowing me to continue with my complaint to the Supreme Court of Canada and still be entitled to my education leave. I couldn't believe it. My decision to reject the agreement had not been a tactic. I believed I was leaving university. Here was a victory for sticking to what I believed was right. I was so quiet listening that he was not sure I was still on the phone.

The next day was October 31, 1985, and P.D. Fitzmaurice travelled to North Bay—by plane!—to have the revised agreement signed. When I heard he was coming so quickly and by plane, I knew they were taking this seriously.

The agreement allowed me three years of paid leave with tuition and books, a job anywhere in the federal public service except National Defence at the end of the three years at the same salary level, and if the new job required a move, all my relocation costs would be covered. It also required me to give up my right to damages against Dennis Brennan, who was no longer an employee of National Defence, to give up my section 45 complaint regarding retaliation, and two other union-related complaints. It stated that I had to agree not to go back to court for damages. The document was then provided to me to sign. I was happy that I could get my education and still go to Supreme Court, but I didn't like the wording that seemed to communicate that after six years of intense struggle I would just give up. I retyped the document myself and added at the end that I was giving up my right to damages as a requirement of the agreement. My good friend Grace signed it as witness. My lawyer did not like my changes, but I stayed firm and told him that this was the only one he was going to get.

The agreement also stated that if I succeeded at the Supreme Court level, I would also agree to drop my right to damages against National Defence. Basically, the agreement ended any opportunity to sue for damages if I was successful. It was a secret agreement with a null-and-void clause if I made the agreement public. At this point I also asked my lawyer to represent me in Supreme Court. I almost wanted to cry because I felt forced into the signing of the agreement and, as I had done my part to sign, I hoped that my lawyer would do his to represent me. He said yes.

COMMITTED TO UNIVERSITY

I proceeded to sort out my commitments at university and finally invested in school both psychologically and practically, now being able to purchase my required textbooks.

The year that followed was very healing. I got good marks, reflecting the hard work I did, and achieved a new peace of mind. I was relieved I could study without having to worry about all the costs associated with university. I was being given credit for what I had achieved. At home, I had time to be with the kids, cook meals, and not have every conversation be about the complaint. A great weight came off my shoulders.

By the end of summer 1986, I decided to make enquiries as to why there had been no word of the complaint proceeding to the Supreme Court. My lawyer assured me everything was progressing normally. In September, I made more follow-up calls with little better results, and by the end of October it was rumoured the Justice Department was working to have the case stricken because there was no money left to argue and the case was arbitrary.

I was getting worried by this time. I was *still* having roadblocks put in my path. I wrote the negotiator with my concerns and said I would invoke the null-and-void clause in the agreement and go back to work at National Defence if I had to. I had signed that agreement on the basis that there would be no interference with my right to proceed to the Supreme Court of Canada.

There were several letters back and forth in November and December 1986, among all parties, discussing whether or not the appeal would be heard. In the end, it was agreed that my appeal would be heard.

II

Supreme Court Victory

O N JANUARY 6, 1987, LARRY AND I TRAVELLED TO OTTAWA FOR the preliminary hearing before the Supreme Court. Even though I was not allowed to attend, I wanted to be there. We travelled again to Ottawa for the May 6 hearing of the case. This time we were in the court. Seven Supreme Court judges were chosen to hear the case, including two women, Justice Bertha Wilson and Justice Claire L'Heureux-Dubé. K. Scott McLean and Michael L. Phelan represented me. We were another step closer to resolving my complaint.

THE LAST WIN WAS THE BEST WIN

After the hearing we waited, again. Waiting was something that happened a lot. Then we heard that the Supreme Court of Canada would make their ruling on July 29. Larry and I again went to Ottawa. We arrived the day before and stayed at a billet. It had taken such a long time to get to this point, and this was the last chance.

Finally, it was the big day. The ruling came down. The Supreme Court of Canada ruled unanimously, finding the employer—the Department of National Defence—vicariously liable for the discriminatory acts of an employee, known or otherwise.

Finally. A huge victory.

The ruling applied to all federally regulated workplaces. (Regulations governing provincially regulated workplaces would be pressured to catch up over time.) Justices Dickson, McIntyre, Lamer, Wilson, Le Dain, La Forest, and L'Heureux-Dubé were present, with Justice La Forest concluding with the disposition, "For these reasons I will allow the appeal, reverse the decision of the Federal Court of Appeal, and restore the decision of the Review Tribunal."

Larry and I were present at the Supreme Court, on Wellington Street in Ottawa, when the verdict was read. I was thrilled to hear the Justice read the decision. I made sure I got a copy of the decision while I was in court and was given it without having to pay the five-dollar fee.

When I asked for a copy, I was proud to say that I was the complainant in the decision, and the clerk was happy to give me a copy.

I felt like I was floating on air! A unanimous decision from all seven judges. We were all elated and we carried that spirit into the following press conference. It was such a tremendous relief. I was excited that I finally had received a decision that I could be proud of and that couldn't be appealed. We had reached the highest court in Canada.

Dr. Marguerite Ritchie arranged a press conference, where she took the lead, explaining that an employer could no

Toronto Star, "Victory at Last," July 30, 1987. Bonnie and Larry in Ottawa, after the Supreme Court victory.

longer ignore sexual harassment at the workplace. When it came to my turn to speak, I said that there was nothing they could have given me, money or otherwise, that was more important than this decision. It was the best ever and I felt ten feet tall!

In the evening, Dr. Ritchie had a wonderful celebratory party at her home, where I met Lucie Laliberté who became instrumental in my representation at the Review Tribunal for damages just over a year later.

I was so excited by the decision I wanted every student from grade 8 and up to receive a copy of it. I wanted everyone to know times were changing and, particularly, that women were gaining some rights when it came to a situation of sexual harassment at work.

Human Rights Review Tribunal, November 1988, from left to right, Marguerite Ritchie, Viva Moulton, Lucie Laliberté, Larry Robichaud, Bonnie Robichaud, and Marguerite Russell

The last win was the best win.

* * *

Larry and I were happy, and I felt confident that National Defence would honour their agreement and I would get paid my wages. We felt that we were now free to take some steps toward a future. While in Ottawa for the ruling, we decided to go house hunting and made an offer on one, without conditions, in Osgoode, a small town forty kilometres outside the city. One month later, our house in North Bay was sold, and we were living near Ottawa in time for the children to enrol for school, September 1987, and I could finish my degree at the University of Ottawa. I wanted to have some control over where I would be working, and what better place than the public service capital of Canada? I knew I could not get a government job in North Bay, and the agreement meant I could be sent anywhere. I was not going to take that chance. Moving to Ottawa was the right thing to do.

While in Ottawa, I also decided to go ahead with a complaint to the Review Tribunal for damages. I asked McLean if he would represent me, and he said no and felt he could not—considering what he knew about the agreement. I accepted his answer. He was a very competent and skilled lawyer, and I am thankful for his work. Before he left my case, he set up the Review Tribunal hearing and turned over to me all the transcripts and other documentation relating to my complaint. My decision to proceed with damages was important for many reasons: It made public the secret agreement, of October 31, 1985, regarding not suing or pursuing my other complaints, and it brought out the actual financial cost of pursuing a complaint. I also had it in mind that if my procedure cost the government a lot of money, they might be more willing to resolve complaints of sexual harassment before they went this far.

SETTLING DOWN IN OTTAWA

My three-year education agreement still had over a year left until it finished, but I was very conscious that after that I had to find a job. I had already been in touch with the Public Service Commission, at which point I found out that I would be competing with eight hundred employees on the priority list. I wanted to be sure I got a job. I followed up with my contact at the Public Service Commission every two weeks either by phone or by visiting her in downtown Ottawa. Each of these visits, phone calls, and letters had to be followed up by more of the same.

The inevitable finally happened, and one day my relationship with National Defence came to an end. I don't remember getting a pink slip in the mail, although I still have the one for June 7, 1985, when I was suspended without pay. All I remember is that while I was working for Labour Canada through an employment agency, I got a phone call from the human resources person at CFB North Bay asking if I wanted my pension money refunded. I said no, to keep it invested. This call didn't signal the end of my employment with National Defence. I was without pay for approximately five months, officially on leave without pay.

Finally, a job became available with Public Works Canada as a building services officer, and I started in late April 1989. When I got there, I found a situation that was similar to my beginnings at CFB North Bay, and once again life was difficult. There were only men in the job, and one of them was a man who had been at CFB North Bay when I made my complaint. He was upset that I was now working in the same office with him.

Training on the job was limited, and the one man who was willing to do some training with me was also willing to demand sexual favours. I complained about this to the Public Service Commission there and was told, "you are allowed to make only one sexual harassment complaint a lifetime," so I got no help there. The head of building services said that so-and-so would not do that and "he is a gentleman." I said, "He is not doing it to you, he is doing it to me." I was offered a transfer to another office, but as there were only four offices and because of the difficult position I was in, I knew that I would soon have nowhere to go and would be out of a job.

As long as I was working on my first complaint, I couldn't mount another full-scale complaint. And I was still on probation. It took another couple of years before I could get this harasser off my back. Eventually, other management in my district office took action to keep him away from me. I had thought that what I had already gone through would have protected me from being sexually harassed again. It did not. It made me an easy target.

I had been required to take this position on a term basis. What I didn't know, though, was that when my term was over, my probation would be extended another six months. I later learned that National Defence continued to pay my wages while Public Works Canada decided if they were willing to hire me when my term ended. This was complicated by my family's move. We had moved to Ottawa from Osgoode the day my term ended, meaning that my address changed. The job offer letter was sent to my old address. I had given my supervisor at Public Works Canada my new address but it doesn't seem to have made it to personnel—at least not in time. Even though I did not have confirmation of a job offer, I decided to keep showing up to work. Luckily, there was a meeting on the fifth day after the end of my term where I was to sign the agreement accepting my position. My co-workers congratulated me on being hired. This was the first I heard of the offer. After the meeting, I was quickly in touch with personnel!

I liked my job at Public Works, not least because I got to see most of the offices of government bureaucrats who had something to do with my complaint. I was paid more to ensure that someone else did cleaning than what I had been paid when I did the cleaning myself, and nobody followed me around. I loved working in Ottawa, and the job was a natural advance from the one I had in North Bay. I had other consequences, though, left over from the working conditions at North Bay. I didn't realize how traumatized I was. I worried unreasonably about my job security, about what was written on my job evaluations, and was constantly concerned about the possibility of being fired. To combat this, I took full advantage of the Employee Assistance Program, which provided employees with counselling when things were overwhelming. These resources were a great help to me when I needed them and made a big difference to my mental health.

SEEKING DAMAGES

Before I had started my job at Public Works, while I was still on leave, I had begun working on my complaint to the Review Tribunal for damages. My first job had been to find a lawyer, since McLean had declined to take it on. The first lawyer I approached laughed at me and said I had had my day in court. The second lawyer I asked had little knowledge of how federal public servants were governed. I didn't have the money for her to learn at my expense.

The third lawyer I hired took the complaint in late November 1987. On the advice of another lawyer, I had the hearing postponed until April 1988, but by then, my lawyer had taken another assignment and was unable to continue.

Amid this discouraging lack of progress, I was busy on a project that came out of a conference I attended in 1982 on women's issues in the workplace, organized with the support of the Ontario Department of Labour. After the conference, I had received a follow-up letter from the Ontario Women's Directorate that was a call for submissions for relevant projects. Recognition was growing that sexual harassment in the workplace was a big problem, and I was willing to talk about what happened to me *and* I was fighting it in court, making my experience unusual and valuable. Based on this, I had submitted a proposal for a booklet about sexual harassment in the workplace and what you could do about it. My proposal was successful and right around this time, in 1988, I used the grant I received of three thousand dollars to write, print, and distribute one thousand booklets titled *A Guide to Fighting Workplace Sexual Harassment/Assault*. Writing and publishing this booklet was an empowering moment. I was able to share what I was learning with others, and maybe make a difference to someone else in a similar situation.

A Guide to Fighting Workplace Sexual Harassment/Assault written, printed, and distributed by Bonnie in 1988. In 1996, PSAC printed more copies in English and, for the first time, in French..

In 1994, because of demand, I did a reprint at my own expense and, two years later, my booklet was translated into French and copies in English and French were printed by the Public Service Alliance of Canada, making copies available to an even wider audience.

*   *   *

My search for a lawyer to take on my complaint for damages was also, finally, successful. I was introduced to Marguerite Russell, a feminist and barrister from England, through Lucie Laliberté, who I met at my Supreme Court celebration party. Russell and I spent the summer of 1988 preparing the case, the broadest argument to date with respect to human rights legislation. Costs were estimated at $161,000, to recover expenses and the hundreds of hours of work necessary to bring my case to its successful conclusion and put an end to the discriminatory practices, and Russell asked for all of them. We asked for the maximum that could be awarded at the time, $5,000. Up to the time of my appeal, the full amount had never been awarded. Sadly, on the evening before the hearing, Marguerite Russell's mother passed away in England, and she had to return to look after her mother's affairs. Again, the hearing had to be postponed.

The hearing for damages finally started on November 28, 1988. The first hurdle to overcome was to establish that the Tribunal had the jurisdiction to hear my case. It had been six years since these tribunal members had made a decision in my case. In that time their appointments had lapsed. It took two hearing days for the lawyer representing National Defence, Donald Rennie, to accept the Human Rights Commission's jurisdiction on behalf of the Crown. National Defence tried to make a case for hearing the Human Rights Commission's case without hearing from me, but the Tribunal made it clear that they were inseparable. (As was true throughout my court appearances, right from the beginning, while working for National Defence and then for Public Works, except for the time when I was on leave without pay, all court hearing days were paid to me as paid leave.)

In these first few days, the Tribunal ruled that a person cannot sign away their human rights by private contract. This was significant. It meant that the secret agreements commonly signed by worn-out complainants of sexual harassment could not be used to interfere with their human rights.

At least fourteen witnesses appeared during the Tribunal hearings, which lasted a total of thirteen days—three days in November, five days in January and February 1989, and five days in June and July. This broken-up schedule was similar to all of my hearings (except at the Supreme Court, which was only one day) and, again, I was left under oath (as in the first Tribunal). Between the November adjournment and the restart in January, I was unable to speak to the media, produce my newsletter, or talk with my lawyer Marguerite Russell.

On January 30, 1989, the hearing resumed. The following days were grueling ones for me. I was called to the stand to resume cross-examination no less than five times, and finally on day seven, I had had enough. When Rennie, the National Defence's lawyer, asked me if the rest of the cleaning staff might be jealous of my opportunity to go to university, I broke down. I answered that I had been gotten rid of and that I did not want to let my peers know that I had been kicked out like a dog. After only a few more questions, I was able to step down, exhausted but relieved. I was no longer under oath. Finally, I could speak to my representative, Marguerite Russell.

During the hearings, National Defence did their best to convince the tribunal members that the Department of National Defence had a reasonable plan for dealing with complaints about sexual harassment and had introduced effective education for employees about their human rights and, in particular, regarding sexual harassment. For example, Larry Richardson, an instructor at the training school, CFB Kingston, testified about his knowledge of what kind of training military personnel were receiving in relation to handling a complaint of sexual harassment. Through the course of his testimony, it was found that National Defence had virtually no standing orders in place to deal with the problem. The training provided by Captain Richardson was what he initiated on his own, because he felt that sexual harassment was a serious problem. A witness from the Human Rights

Commission noted that the Human Rights Commission provided educational seminars about the problem of sexual harassment across the country. For example, he noted that CFB North Bay was given a one-hour seminar, October 30, 1985, the day before I had signed my agreement with National Defence. This was the first I had heard of it!

There was a lot of time spent going over my expenses, with National Defence claiming, somehow, that I should owe them money. That was not the opinion of the Tribunal.

One very significant first happened early in the hearings that would benefit victims of sexual harassment in future cases. Constance Backhouse, author with Leah Cohen, of *The Secret Oppression: Sexual Harassment of Working Women*, the first book about sexual harassment to be published in Canada, testified as an expert witness—the first time a Tribunal in Canada had accepted an expert witness relating to sexual harassment.

Since I was no longer under oath, newsletters nine and ten, with news of the hearings, were produced and distributed.

REVIEW TRIBUNAL: DETERMINATION HONOURED

On December 21, 1989, the Review Tribunal rendered a decision. I was awarded the maximum allowed of five thousand dollars for hurt feelings and a written apology that would be posted at all National Defence facilities around the world, in both French and English. The decision did not set out a work plan to deal with discrimination nor did it deal with my expenses. It said the agreement I signed on October 31, 1985, saying I would not sue for damages was valid and binding. It did confirm that I was able to claim moving costs to my new job in Ottawa, as it was part of the agreement. The Tribunal decision also recognized that my new job reflected my increased education and this was the reason I was receiving higher pay than what the agreement specified.

I was very happy with the wording of the Tribunal's decision:

> In determining the amount of the award, the Tribunal has considered the following factors. In particular: a) the singling out of Mrs. Robichaud by downgrading her job responsibilities; b) the failure to monitor Brennan's conduct to prevent him from attempting to influence witnesses before the Tribunal of the first instant; c) the failure to prepare both Robichaud and her fellow employees for her return to work two days after Brennan's dismissal; and d) the failure, even to this date, to offer an unequivocal apology to Mrs. Robichaud.
>
> We feel compelled to comment on one aspect of these proceedings which disturbed us. It appeared that the Human Rights Commission, following upon the decision of the Review Tribunal, did not provide the degree of support and assistance to the complainant that we would have expected. In fact, it was clear that had it not been for Mrs. Robichaud's determination, this matter would not even have proceeded to the Supreme Court of Canada, much less have been returned to this Tribunal. We do not believe that the public interest has been adequately served in this regard.

I was glad to receive the five thousand dollars, knowing it was the maximum allowed at the time. I sent a letter expressing my fervent thanks to the five women who helped with my legal case and shared some of the money with them: Marguerite Russell (who worked pro bono on my case), Viva Molton, Lucie Laliberté, Sarah Salter, and Marguerite Ritchie.

I was unhappy not to be awarded interest (which was 18 per cent at the time) and annoyed the government also deducted almost six hundred in income tax and Canada Pension Plan and Employment Insurance contributions. I phoned a contact at National Defence and gave them an earful, explaining that the five thousand dollars was not taxable and that I was owed five thousand and not a penny less. That money was refunded to me with a nasty letter.

MOVING FORWARD

I had spent more than ten years under enormous stress, often being humiliated and then reliving the humiliation at every new hearing. I was not quite ready to let it all go, and I decided to take the case for compensation one step further. When all was said and done with the Review Tribunal for damages, I had my moving costs paid, the five thousand dollars for pain and suffering, and my job secured, but I was still not comfortable with all the expenses that were paid out of our family income. I was angry at everything it had taken to get here, and I felt that I owed myself and my family one last attempt to get back some of it.

The agreement I signed with the Treasury Board (for National Defence) stated that if I needed to be relocated outside North Bay for my new job, that "any expenses to be incurred because of such relocation will be paid by the employer." I couldn't see why this wouldn't include compensation for the higher cost of living in Ottawa compared to North Bay, a cost that was necessary as a result of relocating to the Ottawa area to maintain employment. With the support of the Public Service Alliance of Canada, who paid the legal fees, I proceeded to the next and final step in the court ladder. My lawyer asked that I be fully compensated for the difference in the cost of housing.

After only one day of hearings, I lost. Apparently, the agreement I made with the Treasury Board was as per Treasury Board policy and, as such, did not allow for this claim, something I had not understood and was not clear through reading the agreement. I was disappointed with the decision and felt badly about the expense of the legal fees I had put my union through.

But now I was ready to stop. I decided it was time to look forward. Time to celebrate. I decided I would celebrate for a full year. I was celebrating my being of sound mind and body and for having the love of my family. When that year was over, I decided that was not enough. This time I decided to celebrate for the rest of my life, for still being of sound mind and body after over eleven years of struggle in the courts. Even with the continuous and tremendous obstacles I have faced, I have persevered and triumphed. I am not just a survivor.

I WAS THE SOLUTION, NOT THE PROBLEM

When I now think of my struggle, I find it is a miracle that I ended up working for the federal government for twenty-seven years. I got to keep the job that was important to me: A good job, with a good salary, and good working conditions.

I continued to be involved in the fight against sexual harassment by being a board member of the Human Rights Institute of Canada under the leadership of Dr. Marguerite Ritchie. After I retired, I became an honorary member of Groupe d'Aide et d'information sur le harcèlement sexuel au travail and for over eleven years I drove to Montreal to participate in their board meetings. I participated in the creation of the national group against sexual harassment in the workplace. I spoke in schools in Ottawa and provided the students with information flyers about sexual harassment.

I made a difference and lived to tell you my story. To do so, I had to reach out of my comfort zone. To gain support, I became a feminist advocate, a public speaker, a volunteer. I travelled across Canada and spoke to women's groups, schools, unions, and conferences.

My story is not one I would wish on anybody, but when I look back, I can see my strength and how it grew. I opened up doors that never would have been opened. I got the chance to meet incredible women from coast to coast. I became part of a movement that matters, that changes things, that made working situations better for all the women who came after me. I helped open up a space for other women to speak up. Out of our work, came the #MeToo movement of today. I am proud of my part in change and happy to be continuing my influence through this book. Has the struggle been worth the effort? Yes.

Writing this book has been very difficult and rewarding at the same time. Out of the writing, I have come to better understand what I always knew—that it was never my fault. I worked in an unsafe workplace environment.

I was not the problem.

AFTERWORD

I AM VERY GRATEFUL FOR WHAT THE UNION HAS DONE FOR ME AND the role it has played in my life. But before I go on, it is important to also remember that it took four years to get the help I was asking for from the union, four long years that many without my persistence would not have been able to sustain. I often had to pay legal fees from my own pocket before I was able to get their support. A major barrier in my being able to access help was the policy of not helping a member who was grieving against another member. Many times, the harasser benefited from my local not helping me, and this has been true for many others, members who were disadvantaged by not getting help when the grievance was against another member. Thank goodness this policy has been changed.

It was a long four years I had to fight to get the help I so desperately needed from my union. Now I have the union support for which other members can benefit if persistent enough.

* * *

"Alliance wins major sexual harassment case. This tremendous victory which cost thousands of dollars and untold hours of work done and paid for by Sister Robichaud and her agents, now benefits all its members and workers across Canada," states an article in the Public

Service Alliance of Canada's *Union Update*, January 19, 1990. I could not have made this major achievement without the legal fees paid for by the Public Service Alliance, and I will always be thankful for their support.

On November 3, 1990, I was elected first vice-president of my new local, where my job was to handle grievances. Back in November 1978, when I was elected second vice-president at my previous local, I had not expected a twelve-year gap between the two positions. Still, no one could claim I had not been active in the union in the meanwhile. I now came to this position with an enormous amount of knowledge and experience, helping lead to success in the grievance process. I put a proposal forward in a union management meeting that our cleaners be allowed to take part in the BEST program (Basic Education Skills Training), which ran for about four years at Public Works Canada, and I was one of the instructors. I remained active as a union member and in my local until I retired in December 2004 and even after. I was elected to my local executive for all but one year and even then I attended the executive meetings. I was honoured to have been made a life member of Government Services Union and the Public Service Alliance of Canada.

Upon retirement, I was given a steak dinner party, where I was honoured with congratulations from my colleagues for the contributions I made at work and presented with a gift certificate. Women are now working as building services officers and getting respect equal to that of men. I also received a large and supportive retirement party.

My union now respects me for the complaint I struggled to make public and bring successfully through the courts. I am treated with respect by my union sisters and brothers and I feel valued and welcome. I could not have succeeded were I not a union member, and they are continuing to support me. The Public Service Alliance of Canada is helping to have my story told.

Government Services Union honoured me with a "Bonnie Robichaud" board room at the Ottawa headquarters at 233 Gilmour Street and there is a union scholarship in my name.

I am still married to the same man I married in August of 1966. My children have all grown and lead productive lives, and I have nine grandchildren and one great-grandson, at the time of writing. I am very happily retired, and live in a senior's residence where I pursue my hobbies of sewing, crafts, reading, writing, and travel. I also enjoy it when some of the young people who work here ask me to tell my story. At least one has continued with extra research to make a school presentation. I want young people to know that it's possible to stand up for your rights and make a difference. It's hard work. But it's possible.

After she retired, Claire L'Heureux-Dubé (left), the first woman from Quebec appointed to the Supreme Court, accepted the nomination of honorary member of GAIHST at their 25th anniversary, presented to her by Bonnie.

ACKNOWLEDGEMENTS

I'LL BEGIN BY THANKING MY BOOK WRITING TEAM, HEADED BY Penny Bertrand, who, along with Richie Allen, began the process by picking up the twenty-three boxes of documents and transcripts from my home to bring to the Public Services Alliance of Canada's headquarters. Then, with Richie Allen's contacts, they arranged to have my documents placed at Library and Archives Canada. And once there, thank you Dalton Campbell, archivist, for the massive job of making sense of my twenty-three boxes. And finally, together, they found a publisher, Between the Lines, to whom I am so grateful.

Without Yvonne Séguin this project would not have been completed. She inspired me to continue writing even when I was very discouraged, and she supported me throughout the years.

At a crucial point in the process of turning this project into a published book, Heather Weinrich encouraged many busy people to provide their valuable comments on what the Supreme Court of Canada decision meant to the fight against sexual harassment. Many of these comments can be found in the appendix to this book. Thank you Heather for taking care that these came through and to those who wrote on my behalf, including, the Honorable Claire L'Heureux-Dubé (whose comments became the book's preface), Andrew Raven, Jane Stinson, Larry Robichaud, Cindy Viau, Constance Backhouse, Wendy McPeake, Michèle Rivet (and Leyla Chaachay, who did the translation), Rosemary Warskett, Sharon Scrimshaw, and, always, Yvonne Seguin.

Thank you to the focus group that read my manuscript and gave me valuable feedback, Mélisande Masson, Claudine Lippé, and Nathalie Laflamme. A big thank you to Bob Allen for being there for the Workers History Museum and to the Workers History Museum for fundraising and paying the bills on the path to turning my writing into this book. To Maria Thomas, from Public Service Alliance of Canada, for helping me update my union information in the last stages of writing.

Mary Newberry, my wonderful editor, who made everything make sense.

My friend in North Bay, Grace Hucul, for being there first. Marie McNeely, for being there when no one else in the union was during those first critical months. And the Ontario Federation of Labour, for helping me start the Bonnie Robichaud Defence Committee and all those who worked on it. The Public Service Alliance of Canada for their major sponsorship of this book and for lifting me up by paying my legal fees and reimbursing what I had already paid. Daryl Bean, for being there once Public Service Alliance of Canada gave its support and for successfully advocating for their continued support.

The law students and volunteers from the Help and Information Center on Sexual Harassment in the Workplace (GAIHST) were invaluable and enthusiastic and did all and any research that was asked for or that I needed. So many dedicated women's groups and unions supported my struggle with donations and supportive letters. Thank you to the many media people who reported my struggle.

My lawyer K. Scott McLean, who with confident professionalism, represented me all the way to my win at the Supreme Court of Canada, without which this would be an entirely different story. Marguerite Russell, Dr. Marguerite Ritchie, Lucie Laliberté, Viva

Molton, and Sarah Salter worked tirelessly on the Review Tribunal for damages.

Government Services Union thank you for believing in me. To Public Works and Government Services Canada for welcoming me and never making me feel I was the problem.

Thank you Larry, my husband of fifty-five years, for doing all you could to move forward and never complaining about the cost or my being away from home; and to my children, who had a part-time mom.

Finally, thank you to all those too numerous to name, who have helped in big and small ways throughout this long journey.

APPENDIX

RESOURCES

Bonnie Robichaud's records are kept at Library and Archives Canada. To see a listing of the collection, visit the Library and Archives Canada, Collection Search, "Bonnie Robichaud."

All of the decisions in Bonnie Robichaud's cases are also available online.

For the Canadian Human Rights Tribunal decisions, navigate to the decisions page on the Tribunal's website, and in the search box, enter the codes listed below.

1. Canadian Human Rights Tribunal, Robichaud v. Brennan, June 30, 1982: TD6/82
2. Canadian Human Rights Review Tribunal, Robichaud v. Brennan, February 21, 1983: TD4/83
3. Canadian Human Rights Review Tribunal, Robichaud v. Brennan, December 21, 1989: DT18/89
   Commentary and a detailed explanation of the decision, sponsored by Groupe d'aide et d'information sur le harcèlement sexuel au travail de la province de

Québec (GAIHST), can be found on their website:
www.gaihst.qc.ca/bonnierobichaudresearch
4.   Federal Court of Appeal, Brennan v. Canada and Robichaud,
     February 18, 1985: Brennan v. Canada and Robichaud (1985) 57
     N.R. 116 (FCA)
5.   Supreme Court of Canada, Canadian Human Rights, Robichaud
     v. Canada (Treasury Board), July 29, 1987–SCC Cases: 19344
     19326
6.   Federal Court, Robichaud v. Canada (Attorney General), January
     7, 1991: Action no. T-2028-90

COMMENTARY ON CONTEXT AND IMPACT

Constance Backhouse
*Legal scholar, internationally known for feminist research and
publications on sex discrimination and the legal history of gender and
race in Canada.*

I think it is critically important to acknowledge the pivotal role
that Bonnie Robichaud played in our struggles to eradicate sexual
harassment.

Her complaint to the Canadian Human Rights Commission in
1980 set in motion a landmark case that stretched all the way up to
Canada's top court. Our legal system had grievously failed to recognize sexual harassment as a legal injury before, but Bonnie Robichaud
knew that she had been injuriously harmed, and that the law must
respond.

All too often, we can forget that individual women stand at the threshold of these world-changing legal struggles. We miss reflecting upon what it takes to mount such a challenge.

The process is aptly characterized as "naming, blaming, and claiming."

"Naming" is the first component, and one that took on particular significance in this case. Although women have been sexually coerced and assaulted in the workforce for centuries, it was not until April 1975, that the term "sexual harassment" was first coined in Ithaca, New York. There a group of feminists, struggling to name this pervasive problem, held a meeting and dismissed phrases such as "sexual abuse," "sexual intimidation," and "sexual exploitation on the job" and issued a press release calling for an end to "sexual harassment." Within months, the term spread as feminists across the United States and Canada latched onto it in deep recognition of the symbolic force of a new name. By the late 1970s, the new term reached Bonnie Robichaud in North Bay, and she chose the label to describe her excruciating experiences as a cleaner at the Department of National Defence. She was not going to remain silent. She was ready to call her treatment for what it was.

"Blaming" is the second component, and here Bonnie Robichaud's visionary ideas are clearly evident. The key to transformative change is to blame the individual or institution responsible, the party who has the capacity to eradicate the behaviour. Generations of women had pointed the finger inwardly, blaming themselves, shaming themselves for provoking unwanted sexual attention. Instead, Bonnie Robichaud bravely pointed the finger outwardly, at the supervisor who had forced his sexual assaults upon her. And she didn't stop there. She also blamed the governmental department that employed them both. She understood that the resolution of the problem required more than holding one individual at fault. The federal government must also shoulder responsibility for eliminating sexual harassment in its workplace.

"Claiming" was the final component in this path-breaking case.

Bonnie Robichaud took on the demanding, intensive, time-consuming task of calling to account her supervisor and her governmental employer for the injury to her sexual autonomy and self-respect. That laborious process required year after year of legal wrangling, layer upon layer of appeals, and bearing witness in front of innumerable sympathetic and unsympathetic investigators, adjudicators, and judges. The financial cost, the reputational danger, the emotional devastation, and the public exposure were incalculable.

Bonnie Robichaud shouldered all of this, not just on her own behalf, but on behalf of all Canadian women. It was a gigantic personal sacrifice in pursuit of a remarkable demand—that all women be free from coercive sexual harassment in the future.

For this, Bonnie Robichaud will be someone whose name and story remains permanently embossed in Canadian history. For her years of courageous struggle, her ultimate legal victory, and her belief that women deserve equality, we thank her.

Michèle Rivet

Law professor, judge of the Quebec Youth Court, president and founder of the Quebec Human Rights Tribunal, and lawyer (among many other things)

BONNIE ROBICHAUD: A PIONEER WHO HAS PERMANENTLY MARKED THE HISTORY OF THE VICTIMS OF HARASSMENT IN CANADA
Translation by Leyla Chaachay

Thank you Bonnie!!!

The Human Rights Tribunal was established in Quebec in 1990. I was its first president, holding the position until 2010. The right to equality was still in its infancy; article 15 of the Canadian Charter had only been in force since 1985. At the Human Rights Tribunal, we were well aware of the importance of the Canadian Supreme Court's judgments in this regard, even though, they were about questions that initially emerged from other provinces.

This is how Bonnie Robichaud has marked the history of the Human Rights Tribunal of Quebec. In numerous judgments—it would be too long to list them all—we have applied the law that Bonnie Robichaud helped to establish by her long battle to the Canadian Supreme Court. Bonnie, we thank you!

We could never highlight enough the importance of Bonnie Robichaud's long battle in such trying work conditions, in order to establish the employer's liability for an employee's harassing behaviour, which is now acknowledged and seems obvious. But such was not the case until Bonnie undertook her long journey to the Canadian Supreme Court.

We have to remember that jurisprudence, before this, only acknowledged the employer's liability in cases where there was an express mention in the law. This approach, which was largely that of many courts of appeal in Canada, was even followed by a majority of the Federal Court of Appeal in the case of Bonnie Robichaud (Treasury Board c. Bonnie Robichaud, (1985) 6 C.H.R.R. D/26950) where, as we know, the issue of the employer's liability was raised, in this case a federal ministry, for the sexual harassment perpetrated by an employee-supervisor. This is how Federal Court judge Furlow expressed it:

> In my opinion, there is no basis in law for applying such a concept. [. . .] nothing in the wording purports to impose on employers an obligation to prevent or to take effective measures to prevent employees from engaging in discriminatory practices for their own

ends. I see nothing in the section or elsewhere in the status to say that a person is to be held vicariously or absolutely strictly liable in accordance with common law tort or criminal law principles for discrimination engaged in by someone else, whether an employee or not. (D/2703)

Unequivocally, the Canadian Supreme Court overruled this tendency, in 1987, in the Robichaud case (Robichaud c. Canada (Conseil du Trésor), 1987 CanLll 73 (CSC), [1987] 2 R.C.S. 840), where it upheld that the employer is liable for employees' discriminatory practices, whether there is an express mention to that effect in the law or not.

By taking as a starting point "the Act, the words of which [. . .] must be read in light of its nature and purpose"(20), the Court, in fact, establishes that the remedial nature of the Act commands efficient remedies that are compatible with the quasi-constitutional nature of the rights it protects. In regards to discrimination, the importance that is given to the concrete effects of an action, regardless of the author's motives or intentions, prompts the Court to set aside the traditional theories of liability based on fault, and that require the contested act to have been carried out in the course of employment.

It is not a matter of punishing the person who has perpetrated the discrimination but rather to provide victims with a judicial remedy and eliminate all forms of discrimination. For the Supreme Court, the employer's main responsibility is founded on the fact that the law is concerned with the ramifications of discrimination rather than its cause, as Judge La Forest writes:

[. . .] it must be admitted that only an employer can remedy undesirable effects; only an employer can provide the most important remedy—a healthy work environment. (94)

[. . .] It indicates that the intention of the employer is irrelevant [. . .].

After noting the detrimental consequences of a narrower scheme of liability in light of the objectives of the law, the Court outlines the extent of acts for which the employer will be liable, that is: "[. . .] for all acts of their employees in the course of employment, interpreted in the purposive fashion outlined earlier as being in some way related or associated with employment." (95)

At the Human Rights Tribunal, we have applied this Canadian Supreme Court excerpt many times. I will only mention our decision in the Claudine Lippé case in 1998 (Commission des droits de la personne et des droits de la jeunesse (Lippé) v. Québec (Procureur général), 1998 CanLII 30 (QC TDP). It seems like yesterday to me! Claudine was also very brave. . .

Bonnie Robichaud, by her determination, tenacity and resilience has profoundly marked the entire protection that victims of harassment now have a right to in their work place. A fight led by a woman, first and foremost for women, but more broadly for all victims. We all THANK YOU!

An everyday woman with a great destiny.

Andrew Raven
Counsel for the Public Service Alliance of Canada, Review Tribunal, Robichaud v. the Queen

In many ways, Bonnie Robichaud's case was before its time. Looking back today, at a time when sexual harassment in the workplace is squarely in the public eye, it is almost unthinkable that an employer's responsibility and liability for sexual harassment in employment could ever have been in doubt. In 1985, however, only two years before the Supreme Court's decision, the Federal Court of Appeal had held that an employer was only responsible for workplace sexual harassment if a complainant could prove that top officials had been aware of and had authorized or knowingly condoned the conduct.

By rejecting the Federal Court of Appeal's conclusion, the Supreme Court in *Robichaud* paved the way for our modern understanding that employers have significant obligations in terms of ensuring a safe, respectful and harassment-free workplace for their employees. Although *Robichaud* may have only directly applied in federal workplaces, its lasting legal principles regarding the efforts that employers must undertake to prevent and address harassment apply across the country to this day.

In addition to its impact on harassment, *Robichaud* also established the important legal principle that human rights protections in employment generally should not be viewed narrowly. The Supreme Court's decision confirmed that the question of whether or not discriminatory actions occurred "in the course of employment" had to be considered in light of the broader purposes of human rights legislation to identify and eliminate discrimination. There is no doubt that this principle continues to have a significant impact and has allowed human rights advocates since *Robichaud* to expand human rights protections to vulnerable categories of workers who might not otherwise have received protections and to address discriminatory behaviour that might not otherwise have been caught.

I have a distinct recollection, from the time that Bonnie's case was unfolding, of the depth of her commitment to this important issue throughout. I am honoured to have played a very small role in a case that has had such far-reaching impact.

Rosemary Warskett

Former PSAC, senior regional representative, Ottawa/Hull; retired professor, Department of Law & Legal Studies, Carleton University.

I became aware of Bonnie Robichaud's sexual harassment complaint in 1981 when I was a regional representative, in the Ottawa office of the Public Service Alliance of Canada (PSAC). I was working closely with the Women's Committee of the PSAC Ottawa Area Council. Their focus was on raising awareness of gender discrimination in federal workplaces and within the union movement. Many members of the committee were also in the Ottawa chapter of Organized Working Women. This was a feminist organization within the Ontario labour movement. Organized Working Women had formed a Women's Caucus that took equality demands to the Ontario Federation of Labour.

This was a time when challenges to workplace patriarchy were coming from many directions across Canada. In Ontario a series of strikes led by women questioned the view that women were difficult to organize and unwilling to fight for better working conditions and pay. Women on the Fleck Industries picket lines (1978) in Southern Ontario, stood their ground against the provincial police and became the face of working-class feminism (Maroney 1983). Other strikes by women workers took place at Blue Cross, Radio Shack, and mini-Skools (Briskin 1983). In Ottawa, during the 1970s, day care workers, in the Canadian Union of Public Employees (CUPE), organized against privatization of day care. And women at the American Banknote Company went on strike for equal pay for work of equal value. Later in 1980, the fifty thousand–strong PSAC Clerk's (76 per cent female) struck for higher pay, followed by Canadian Union of Postal Workers' (CUPW), which gained paid maternity leave. Both struggles fundamentally altered women's status in federal sector unions and at the bargaining table (Warskett 1996).

Ottawa Area Council's Women's Committee stepped up to take part in challenging unions' patriarchal culture. Women's subordinate position in the workplace was the subject of meetings and forums. Education sessions were held exploring the relation between discrimination and sexual harassment in the workplace, and the power exercised by men in positions of authority. The committee explored the multiple ways that women experienced discrimination in workplaces and linked them to the general subordination of women in society and the home.

Second wave feminism had already brought significant legal changes. Recommendations in 1970 by the Royal Commission on the Status of Women had resulted in the enactment of the Canadian Human Rights Act (CHRA: 1978) with provisions against sex discrimination. The other Canadian Human Rights Act provision that sparked a lot of interest was equal pay for work of equal value. The Women's Committee met with the PSAC classification experts to discuss the meaning of the provision and the possibility of raising the value of women's work. In 1984, PSAC made the equal pay complaint pertaining to federal departments. Eventually it was settled in October 1999.

It was in this context of growing union feminism that members of the Women's Committee met with Bonnie Robichaud. Her treatment by her local union executive demonstrated that changing women's material reality, in the workplace and the union, required a lot more than anti-discrimination provisions in the Canadian Human Rights Act. Putting the law into action would require all of Bonnie's courage and strength, together with mobilizing union women to back her up. Pressure was brought by the women's committee on the PSAC executive to support the case and give money for Bonnie's legal defence.

Women from the committee also gave direct support and billeted Bonnie when she came to Ottawa for meetings. Contact was made with the Toronto Organized Working Women and women in the Ontario Federation of Labour to widen the support network.

When the Canadian Human Rights Tribunal decision was handed down in June 1982 the outcome shocked many of us. The issue of consent was raised in a very graphic way in Richard Abbott's written decision. He wrote that he found Bonnie's testimony very credible, but masturbation and fellatio could not possibly happen without consent. We were stunned. It was as if all the discussions by women during the last twenty-five years had happened in a vacuum. It seemed that the Tribunal members had no understanding of how power relations between a subordinate and supervisor could be used to intimidate, through threats of discipline, demotion, and dismissal, and lead to the coercion of sexual favours.

What also became apparent, through the course of the complaint process, was that PSAC had a representation problem. The local and component represented Dennis Brennan, but no thought or care was given to Bonnie's representation. Eventually, a new PSAC policy concerning alleged harassment by one union member by another was put in place. The policy includes fair hearings and representation that are consistent with the condemnation of harassment, as well as holding the employer to its duty to achieve and maintain a harassment free workplace, in keeping with the Supreme Court of Canada's 1987 decision *Bonnie Robichaud vs. Canada* (PSAC 2008).

Today we are still fighting to remove sexual harassment and discrimination from our workplaces. Bonnie Robichaud's courage in pursuing justice and refusing to be silenced means that the situation in our workplaces is considerably better than it was in the 1980s. But law and legal decisions can remain dead letters unless we give support, representation, and open-minded, non-biased hearings to those

alleging harassment. As well we must continue to advocate for and mobilize in favour of harassment free workplaces together with working for equality in society generally. The struggle continues.
References

›   Briskin, L. (1983), 'Women's Challenge to Organized Labour' in L. Briskin and L. Yanz (eds.) *Union Sisters: Women in the Labour Movement.* Toronto: Women's Press.
›   Maroney, H.J. (1983), 'Feminism at Work.' *New Left Review* No 141.
›   PSAC (2008), PSAC Policy on Union Representation: Workplace Harassment. Adopted by the National Board of Directors. Ottawa.
›   Warskett, R. (1996), 'The Politics of Difference and Inclusiveness within the Canadian Labour Movement.' *Economic and Industrial Democracy: An International Journal*, Vol 17 No. 4.

Wendy McPeake
Women's Committee of the Public Service Alliance

Bonnie came to the attention of the newly formed Women's Committee of the Public Service Alliance in the 1980s. She was a cleaner at the Department of National Defence in North Bay and was severely sexually harassed by her supervisor.

We were shocked and outraged to learn that the union would not provide legal representation for Bonnie even though her harasser, who was her supervisor, was being supported. The union argued that it could not represent her because the union was already representing the harasser. We mobilized women to sign a petition, which was presented to the PSAC President. [These petitions are in the Women's Archives at Ottawa University.] After a meeting with the president, the union agreed to pay for her legal fees. This was a nice victory, but the union local continued to discriminate against her, isolating her in her workplace and kicking her out of the local. It was only through legal actions and union intervention that these actions were reversed.

As Bonnie lived in North Bay and had to travel to Ottawa, I met with her frequently and she stayed in our home. I got to know her amazing resilience and strength in fighting for her rights. Her case was a landmark case for sexual harassment in the workplace and had the effect of encouraging other women to bring their cases forward. Unfortunately, sexual harassment is still rampant today in the Department of National Defence and RCMP. The only encouraging note is that many more women are bringing their cases forward— more than three hundred and fifty women signed on to a class action suit against the RCMP. Tragically, one of the women involved took her life. Only now has National Defence committed itself to a zero tolerance policy, and I believe that Bonnie's case provided a precedent and paved the way for others to come forward, albeit so many years later.

Jane Stinson
Feminist trade union activist in Ottawa

Winning an Uphill Battle: Bonnie Robichaud's courage to say "enough" and report her boss's sexual harassment at work in 1979 started the ball rolling toward a watershed Supreme Court of Canada decision in 1987 that made employers responsible for preventing sexual harassment in federal workplaces.

But this was not a ball rolling along easily to an inevitable con-clusion. No. Bonnie was like the Greek mythological figure, Sisyphus. Except she was a modern-day feminist also pushing a large, heavy rock uphill, for many years, facing and needing to overcome several obstacles along the way. She was forging a path thirty years before the modern #MeToo Movement against sexual harassment.

Bonnie not only stood up to her harasser, but she also had to stand up to her union, to insist that they take her case forward. For the next eight years she had to organize pressure to ensure that they did. Bonnie wrote a 1988 *Guide to Fighting Workplace Sexual Harassment/ Assault* with financial support from the Ontario Women's Directorate. There are sections on "Signs That Show No Support from the Union" and "What to do if You Don't Get Union Support" informed by her personal experiences.

Bonnie organized support among feminist and human rights groups. I recall the important role the PSAC Ottawa-Hull Regional Women's Committee played in mobilizing and demonstrating the broad-based support Bonnie had to their national union leadership. This pressure was needed to convince the union to put financial resources into taking Bonnie's case on for many years and pursuing it to the Supreme Court of Canada.

Bonnie faced many obstacles along the way. Her complaint filed with the Canadian Human Rights Commission in 1980 was dis-missed by the Tribunal, but their decision was overturned on appeal to a Review Tribunal. The Department of National Defence appealed the case to the Federal Court of Appeal, who ruled in 1985. They recognized sexually inappropriate behaviour by her supervisor, but decided that the Department of National Defence, where she worked, was not responsible for sexual harassment unless top officials had con-doned the behaviour. (Clarke, Marc. 1987. No to sexual harassment. *Maclean's*.)

Two years after the Federal Court of Canada loss, her case was upheld by seven Supreme Court of Canada justices. They ruled unanimously that employers in areas under federal jurisdiction are responsible for acts of harassment that their employees commit in the workplace. This Supreme Court of Canada's decision on employer's responsibility for sexual harassment in the workplace sent shock waves across the country, affecting women workers well beyond the federal sector.

A fundamental principal was established, thanks to Bonnie and everyone who got behind her case. Employers are now responsible to provide a workplace free of sexual harassment. Our formal rights, like this one, are only as strong as our ability to enforce them. Working women don't have to put up with this behaviour. We can demand that our employer address it.

Cindy Viau and Yvonne Seguin

Help and Information Centre for Sexual Harassment in the
Workplace/ Groupe d'aide et d'information sur le harcèlement sexuel
au travail de la province de Québec (GAIHST)

Cindy Viau, executive director

Our goal at GAIHST, a non profit community centre dedicated to helping women who are or have been subjected to sexual harassment at work, is to give back power to those who are being subjected to such an abuse of power. We are here to inform them that they have more than the two options that once were dominant, that is, put up with the harassment or quit your job. Bonnie Robichaud's case is one that shows us that it is possible to break the silence. Just like her, many women tell us that they love what they do and that they are good at it, that all they need is for the harassment to stop. But when it does not, what should one do?

This is where the awareness of people who have authority within companies is still crucial; where informed and educated interventions by employers can change the outcome, and how minimizing situations can only make things worse. Bonnie Robichaud's case demonstrates the importance of intervention by those who hold responsibility in work environments, and #MeToo has shown us the same.

We cannot always control what others do and sexual harassment can happen to anyone, but it's not necessarily the sexual harassment that is the problem in itself—the problem is often how the harassment is dealt with. The promotion of safe and respectful workplaces should be a priority for all employers, and Bonnie Robichaud's case put light on this responsibility and its importance.

At GAIHST, we believe that #MeToo was not just a moment, but a movement. And with a movement, comes change. With important judgements, comes change. What does not change, though, is the ever lasting impact on hundreds and thousands of individuals when one decides to stand up, speak up, and be heard.

The impact that Bonnie Robichaud's journey has had on women, workplaces, and different areas of law is long lasting. Many, still today, are benefiting from her courage. The #MeToo Movement is a reminder that we have to keep speaking up and breaking the isolation surrounding sexual harassment at work. There is absolutely no reason for women to have to suffer sexual harassment in workplaces. So, thank you, Bonnie, for lending your voice to many and to have led the way to where we are today.

Yvonne Seguin, founding member

Bonnie and I first crossed paths, when we both had active cases of sexual harassment; we felt an instant connection. Bonnie was unionized and worked for the federal government; I worked in the private sector and did not have union representation. Bonnie's case was before the Supreme Court of Canada and mine was before the Québec Human Rights Commission.

In 1980, I began working at a community centre in Montréal and Bonnie lived in North Bay and travelled to Ottawa to deal with her case. Although far apart, we kept in contact. I promoted the Bonnie Robichaud case in Québec and Bonnie promoted the Help and Information Centre for Sexual Harassment in the Workplace (GAIHST). We did many television and radio programs and conferences together, becoming a two-woman show that supported the struggle against the sexual harassment that plagued many work environments at the time.

The Groupe d'Aide (GAIHST) grew: we began getting more calls and were able to hire more employees. Women from all over Québec were calling and asking for help. Bonnie helped wherever she could, becoming our expert on unionized cases and, based on her case experience with the federal government and her union, she was able to help many of our clients. As a result of her determination and her dedication to the fight against sexual harassment, she proved to women across the country that they could and should speak out. The 1987 Supreme Court unanimous decision, Bonnie Robichaud vs. Canada, affirmed what Bonnie had been saying, that discrimination and sexual harassment are never "part of the Job!" and that employers are liable for the acts of their employees.

Bonnie was our first #MeToo Canadian and an outspoken advocate against verbal abuse of a sexual nature and discrimination, which she pursued all the way to the highest court in Canada. Because of the Court's 1987 ruling , employers today are held responsible for the actions of their employees at work. The judgment of the Supreme Court gave Canadian women the right to be heard regarding inappropriate behaviour based on sex in the workplace, and, for the first time, it had been determined who was responsible. Up to that point nobody was taking responsibility for the harassment, claiming that it was a personal problem between two individuals and not a problem that belonged to the employer. The judgment proved them wrong.

At GAIHST we started immediately receiving phone calls from employers and unions who wanted to hire us for training their employees on what was sexual harassment.

For us at GAIHST, Bonnie became an inspiration: for the clients, for the employees, and for the law students who did placements with us (who considered it a privilege to work with the woman whose case they had studied in their law courses). It was a very rewarding experience for us all.

In 1990 Bonnie became a honorary member of GAIHST and has remained very active with us until her retirement in 2018. Bonnie Robichaud has been one of the driving forces behind our movement in Quebec. She has inspired, encouraged, and supported many women who sought assistance. She has also lobbied with us for our recognition, and her presence on our board of directors has helped to legitimize our purpose to fundraisers, both provincial and federal.

During our professional working lives, Bonnie and I have had the great pleasure of meeting extraordinary women such as justices Claire L'Heureux-Dubé and Michèle Rivet, professors Constance Backhouse, Louise Langevin, and Anita Hill, and thousands of wonderful and creative women who had the courage to say No. Some of them won their cases, some did not, and some cases finished with out-of-court settlements. Every one of those cases laid the groundwork for an empowering trend that brought both women and men toward the #MeToo Movement.

For this reason I can say that what Bonnie started many years ago, the personal struggle of one woman who had the courage to say No and believed in the right to say No, has grown, and I have seen the changes. The most noticeable changes are in the way we look at the workplace environment. In the late 1970s and 1980s women would ask us "Is this sexual harassment?" In 2019 they are telling us, "This *is* sexual harassment." Bonnie Robichaud cleared a path for us to have the right to speak up about what we are being subjected to in our workplace. Sexual harassment should never be "part of the job."

Sharon Scrimshaw
Experienced and fought sexual harassment in the workplace

Bonnie Robichaud, a strong woman ahead of her time.

I first heard the name Bonnie Robichaud when I came forward with a complaint of sexual harassment in the workplace. I experienced this horrible behaviour while working at 3M Canada in London, Ontario. The sexual harassment began five years after I was first employed with 3M, when I was moved to an all-male department in 1979. The harassment continued until I walked out in 1993. At that time you didn't hear or read much about sexual harassment in the workplace so it was a scary endeavour to come forward with a complaint.

Like Bonnie, I also had a union, the Canadian Auto Workers union, now Unifor. When the grievance I submitted pitted union worker against union worker, in the beginning, they really didn't want to grieve my complaint. They only wanted to grieve the men in management who I named, so I felt it necessary to go and seek out a lawyer. That is where I first heard of Bonnie Robichaud. Hearing her name gave me some relief because I felt I wasn't so all alone.

Bonnie was a very brave woman who tackled this issue and went on to the Supreme Court of Canada and won. She started that paved road for women like me. I remember wishing that she lived in London. When you lodge a complaint you feel so alone and vulnerable. A lot of your friends are friends you work with, and they are afraid to contact you because they don't want what you have experienced to happen to them. They don't get involved because they need and want their jobs.

My lawyer told me Bonnie's experiences, and deep down I knew I wanted to meet this woman. She didn't want any more than I wanted, to just go to work, do her job, get paid, and go home. For some women that isn't an option. As with the current #MeToo Movement, most women just kept silent about what happened to them at the time. Women who experienced sexual harassment in the workplace either continued working, dealing in their own way with the harassment, or quit their jobs with no one other than the perpetrators knowing what they were dealing with. This bad behaviour wasn't something at the time people even put a name to because it was common working conditions for so many women.

A lot of women didn't even realize how wrong it was and just dealt with it—they were on their own with children and knew everyone was relying on them financially. We all know going to work every day can be challenging enough.

It takes many years to go through the system with a complaint, and during that time I was lucky to meet Bonnie, in 1998, at a Way Forward Conference we were both speaking at, in London, Ontario. When I first met her I felt I knew her already. When I listened to her speak, I realized she knew what sexual harassment does to you emotionally and how it effects all aspects of your life. It was such a relief knowing someone else knew how you had been feeling for so many years.

Bonnie made my path in the legal system easier for me and also my lawyers—they could use her victory in the courtroom. She made companies sit up and take notice about sexual harassment. The media was picking up on cases and making companies publicly known, and not in a good way. This started people talking about sexual harassment and realizing that what they could be saying or doing in the workplace was harmful and wrong. Training programs around this issue also began.

Women forever should and will be grateful for Bonnie Robichaud's courage, strength, and perseverance on the way to her accomplishments. She is so awe inspiring. Some people choose sports players as heroes. My heroes are strong women like Bonnie Robichaud!

Larry Robichaud
Bonnie Robichaud's husband

When Bonnie first told me what was going on she was a crying mess. I got an appointment for her with a workplace psychologist that afternoon, which gave her a chance to explain what was happening and decide what to do. With the help of the psychologist and Bonnie's regional union representative she put in her grievances.

Bonnie would handwrite many letters, and this is where I was able to help her the most. I reviewed all her written material, and I corrected her spelling and grammar. She would then type it. Later when she started writing the Newsletter I not only corrected the spelling and grammar but helped photocopy them, put the address labels on the envelopes, and filled them. When she travelled out of town for conferences and to meet her lawyer, I stayed home and looked after the children. As I looked after the budget I always made sure that there was enough money to buy the office supplies. I made sure she had someone to talk to when she was very upset by calling her friends who gave her a listening ear.

We worked together to decide how to go forward. I listened to her daily struggles at work and watched her come home discouraged from what was going on.

I helped more with the children as it was too difficult for her during her struggle. I went to the hearings with her whenever possible. When she decided to move to Ottawa I retired from a thirty-four-year service with the provincial government to be with her.

INDEX

Up the Difference, 106; newsletter, 113; support of Robichaud, 108, 111, 171; women's caucus, 169
Ontario Human Rights Commission, 61, 62
Ontario Public Service Employees' Union, 113
Ontario Women's Directorate, 144, 174
Organized Working Women, 169
Ottawa, Ontario: Robichauds' move to, 96, 140, 142, 182. *See also* Canadian Human Rights Commission and Tribunals; Federal Court of Appeal; Supreme Court of Canada
Ottawa Citizen, 125, 127

pamphlets, fighting workplace sexual harassment, 144–45, 174
pension, 141, 149
petitions, 50, 56, 62, 73, 172–73
phone calls: cost of, 96; as part of harassment, 27, 40; received by Robichaud, 121; from Robichaud, 33, 133, 149; between Robichaud and Brennan, 27, 33–34, 35, 37; Robichaud to Marie McNeely, 56
Playboy, 13
probation period, 29–30, 34, 38, 41–44, 60, 98–99, 115, 142
Public Service Alliance of Canada (PSAC): about, 13–14; discrimination and sexual harassment clauses, 111; discussion of tentative agreement, 132, 133; financial support of Robichaud, 102, 118, 149; Marie McNeely, 55; meetings with

Robichaud, 108–9, 112; National Women's Conference, 118–19; Ottawa local, 169, 170, 174; personnel, 102, 106, 108–9; against sexual harassment buttons, 111; representative, 55; sharing Robichaud's cases, 109, 112–13; Sudbury local, 111; support of Robichaud, 70, 102–4, 118, 127; Women's Committee, 101–2, 103, 169, 170–71, 172–73, 174. *See also* grievances and hearings of; Union of National Defence Employees (UNDE)
Public Service Commission, 49, 82, 122–23, 124, 133, 142–43; Anti-Discrimination Directorate, 61, 71–72, 77, 121; and Robichaud's decision to reject National Defence offer, 132–33; women's groups, 79. *See also* Canadian Human Rights Commission and Tribunals
public speaking, 103, 106, 151
Public Works Canada, 106, 141–43
publicity and public awareness: encouragement for Robichaud, 108; growth of, 113; null-and-void clause in tentative agreement, 134; public pressure on National Defence, 129; publication of Robichaud's brief, 106; rise in public support, 101; support during Federal Appeal hearing, 110–11. *See also* Bonnie Robichaud Defence Committee Newsletter; media

Québec Human Rights Commission, 177